Are You d.u.I.?

daily under HIS Influence

101 Questions - A self inventory to help deepen your walk

Jim & Robbie Mihalko

xulon PRESS

Are You d.u.I.?
101 Questions - A self inventory to help deepen your walk
by Jim & Robbie Mihalko

Printed in the United States of America

ISBN 978-1-60791-874-5

www.xulonpress.com

**We dedicate this book to the memory of Jay Scott Duff.
We love you and miss you.**

About The Authors

Jim's Story

I am believer in Jesus Christ who used to struggle with drugs and alcohol and now live daily in freedom at the foot of the cross. I started drinking at age 15 and then started using drugs shortly afterwards. This problem then plagued me for the next 31 years. As you will see from my work history, I had difficulty holding a job once the addiction and alcoholism became full blown. I have made three geographical moves to try and run from my problems. But, everywhere I went, there "I" was. I started to figure out the problem lay deep within me. It wasn't those around me, or "what" was around me.

I am a jack-of-all-trades and master of none. I started my work career in construction. My brother-in-law David, and his brother Wally, gave me a job. Later I changed careers and drove a truck and eventually went into the auto body field. Along the way I have worked at restaurants, delivered pizzas, installed fiber optic cable, chemical sales, auto parts warehouse, Fed-Ex warehouse, delivered phonebooks, delivered flowers, and then back to construction where I heeded the call to full time ministry.

Throughout all this, I married an awesome woman and we had three lovely daughters. God continually kept His hand upon my family. He is faithful that way. As you read through Robbie's comments you will see time and time again how God showed up. Our parents helped out financially, but they could only do so much.

God miraculously removed my desire for drugs and alcohol on January 16th, 2006. Shortly afterwards I was sitting in church one Sunday when I heard God's call. My pastor was speaking about how great it was to get paid to study God's Word and God spoke to me and said "one day you will do that". The seed was planted and 21 months later, d.u.I. ministries was born. d.u.I. ministries is a teaching ministry based on the four pillars of the Christian walk found in Acts 2:42.

Robbie's Story

I dedicated my life to the Lord as a sophomore in high school, and was active in InterVarsity Christian Fellowship in college at Appalachian State University. After college I was a Young Life leader at one of the local high schools in Charlotte, NC and seemed to be doing all the right things, with all the right people, for all the right reasons. I started dating Jim, a non-believer at the time, when I was 24 years old. My head said "no" but my flesh said "yes". I was obviously not walking daily under the influence of the Holy Spirit as I found myself pregnant at the age of 25. Jim and I got married in January 1985 and the roller coaster of our lives together began.

God took something bad and turned it into something amazing, as only He can do. It took faith, perseverance, endless prayer and finally, total surrender. While everyone around me was wondering why I was still with Jim and some even encouraging me to kick him out, God was telling me to endure and trust Him.

Today, our marriage is stronger than most and God has given us this ministry to help encourage others not to give up and not to settle for a mediocre Christian life. God is still in the healing and miracle business. Don't let anyone tell you otherwise.

We have been married since January 1985. We have three daughters, Casey, Corrie, and Jamie. We have recently been blessed with our newest family member Chris (Smiley), Corrie's husband. We worship and serve at Fairview Community Church and live in Fairview, Tennessee.

Acknowledgements

We, first and foremost, want to thank our Lord and Savior, Jesus Christ. Also, our awesome daughters Casey, Corrie, Jamie, and our son-in-law Chris for all their support and prayers. I (Jim) hope the success of this book would make up just a little for all the times I was not there as a father when you were younger. We love you all.

A special thanks to my brother John, one of my best friends, who has been and continues to be, so much help on our website and this book. We would also like to thank the d.u.I. ministries Prayer Partners who are too numerous to list but we are going to anyway: Bill and Susan Bailey, Steve and Sharon Belsheim, Robert and Angie Blanchard, Ed and Joy Bridgman, Perfect Paul and Wonderful Wanda Bullard, Jim and Marcia Coleman, Bud and Nancy Coursey, Keith and Kathy Cribbs, Alan and Eva Curtis, Mark and Lacey Davidson, C.C. and Jeanie Duff, Dave and Andria Duff, John and Andrea Furkins, Tim and Nita Goodman, Brian and Jo Ann Hendrix, Dan and Cheryl Hoover, James and Mary Huette, Ron and Suzanne King, Clint and Dodie Lainhart, Mike and Judy Mangrum, John and Cathy Mihalko, John and Cindy New, "Shot" and Robbie Perrow, David and Lori Polston, Tim and Katie Pulsifer, Curtis and Susan Putnam, Greg and Kim Shelton, Sean and Angela Vereen, Jonathan and Theresa Wehman, and last but most definitely not least Tim and Robin Wood!

We would also like to thank the Northern Mihalko clan. Hey y'all watch this! Word to my (Jim) Tuesday morning Bible study and Thursday night study, thanks for being there. Also thanks to our community group for letting us practice on you!

I (Robbie) would like to thank my dear friend, Marcia and the ladies of Haywood Hills Baptist church for allowing me to share my life and my heart with you.

A big thank you to Fairview Community Church! We love you and thank you for all you have taught us and for helping to bear our burdens.

To our parents, thank you for all you have done. We could never pay you back for your generous support of our family and your standing with us in the tough times.

CONTENTS

Introduction

Our hope and prayer for everyone who reads this book is a fresh look into how to live the Christian life. We know there should be no cookie-cutter Christians. God made everyone an individual with different personalities, talents, gifts, and most definitely looks. But we believe the Bible pretty much spells out how we should be. Once these basics are applied to your life and intertwined with your uniqueness you will see who God really made you to be. We believe once this happens you will know your calling and will be able to live that abundant life God promises and will glorify Him.

We will state up front this is not about "works" we can do for salvation. What we have done is taken verses from the Bible and turned them into questions that you can ask yourself and then see how you stack up against what the Bible says we should be. We know the best counselors are the ones who ask probing questions so that the patient can figure out what is wrong on their own. The only wrong answers are to the salvation questions and our hope is those of you who get them wrong will accept Christ as your Lord and Savoir.

Another reason we wrote this book is we are tired of seeing the church be so ineffective in our society. We believe one of the factors for this is that the church looks no different than the world. What do we have to offer if believers are getting divorced and having abortions at the same rate as the world and every kind of addiction has permeated the church? I am not saying we should be perfect, but I believe we have taken grace to mean license to do whatever we desire. The Bible is quite clear believers have power over sin through the blood of Christ. That power has to be exercised by daily walking with Him. This power comes from the Holy Spirit and if we would just keep the four pillars of the Christian walk from Acts 2:42 (Bible study, fellowship, the Lord's Supper, and prayer.) in balance, we could use that power to be different. The Holy Spirit is no different today than when He was poured out at Pentecost. The early believers changed the world back then and I believe we can too.

We follow each question with a few comments. We try to show in real life experiences how we live out what we teach. Some we fall short on and we are constantly trying to do better so as to serve Him better. We really desire to live that abundant life God promises and glorifies Him. Our prayer is that you and others would also.

If you are a truly born again believer you have the power of the Holy Spirit living in you. All you have to do is learn to yield your flesh to that power. It's not about acting merciful; it's about being merciful. It's not about acting like a prayer warrior; it's about being a prayer warrior. It's not about acting like a Christian; it's about being a Christian! The time to stop acting and start being is now. Our hope is that this book will be a starting point to a powerful and fruitful walk that brings glory to the Father and He will say to you "Well done good and faithful servant". So let's get started with the first ten.

Chapter One

Let's Get Started!

Do You Know The Holy One Of God?

Luke 4:33-34 (Amplified) Now in the synagogue there was a man who was possessed by the foul spirit of a demon; and he cried out with a loud (deep, terrible) cry, Ah, let us alone! What have You to do with us (What have we in common), Jesus of Nazareth? Have you come to destroy us? I know Who You are—the Holy One of God!

Even the demons know Jesus, the Holy One of God. When they meet Him, they cry out in horror as they know He came to destroy them. If you met Jesus face to face would that be your reaction? Or do you have the comfort of knowing Him personally and the fact He came to save that which was lost?

Just knowing the Holy One of God is obviously not enough for salvation. You must believe in Him. The word believe used in the New Testament is the Greek word, pisteuo, which means "to adhere to, to cleave to, to trust; to have faith in; to rely on, to depend on". The demons know Him but they do not "pisteuo" Him.

How is your relationship with the Holy One of God? Do you adhere to His teachings? Do you cleave to His side? Do you trust Him with your life decisions? Do you have faith that He will provide for you? Do you rely on Him daily? Does your salvation depend on what He did and not what you have done? Do you know the Holy One of God?

Robbie's comments:

Yes, I do. He is my Redeemer and my Comforter. I call upon His name and He hears me. Does He always answer the way I would like? Of course not, but there is comfort just knowing that He hears me. Do we always answer our children's cries the way they would like? Of course not. We love them and want only the best for them but sometimes that means giving them an answer that they do not want to hear. Do we always make the right decision? No, but God always makes the right decision. We may not understand it but we can rest assured that it is the right decision. He loves us so and has great and mighty plans for our lives. We must believe that. We must adhere to that and cling to that and believe that with all of our being. We must read our Bible and be involved in a good Bible study so we can grow in our faith and get to know Him more and more. With knowledge comes understanding. It takes time, it takes effort and sometimes even sacrifice but oh, how it will prove to be so worth it!

Jim's comments:

This is one I am sure of. He is absolutely real and has changed my life from a drug addicted alcoholic to a loving father, trustworthy husband, good friend, and faithful servant. I truly know the Holy one of God and my prayer is that you know Him too!

Do You Know The Word?

Hosea 4:6 My people are destroyed for lack of knowledge. Because you have rejected knowledge, I also will reject you from being My priest. Since you have forgotten the law of your God, I also will forget your children.

Here God is speaking to the priests of Israel through the prophet Hosea. He is rebuking them because it was their job to teach the word of God (law) to the people. Part of the problem was that some of the priests themselves had turned from the law and followed after idols. It was an honor and responsibility to teach the people and from the founding of Israel as a nation it was taken seriously. During this period, however, the economy was booming. They were politically, but not spiritually stable. Does that sound familiar?

Do you know the Word? The phrase "to know a man (or woman)" is Biblically used as sexual relations, a very intimate relationship. If you are married, you will know what I am talking about, if not, please wait. Think of your relationship with your spouse or your friends. When you first met it was only superficial knowledge of each other. The only way to get to know each other intimately was to spend time together. It is the same way with God. To get to know Him better, you have to spend time in His Word. It tells us about Him, His attributes, His standards, His likes and dislikes, His love, His fury, His grace and His plan for us.

If your life is troubled or you feel adrift, think about how much time you spend in the Word. Think about all the other things you spend time on or fill yourself with. To know God is to spend time in His Word. It will keep you from being destroyed. Do you know the Word?

Robbie's comments:

Very recently, one of my brothers in Christ, Andy Brucato, had a severe stroke and lay in his home for hours before being discovered. He said that while he was lying there, he just kept quoting Scripture, over and over again. I had to stop and think if that were me, how much Scripture would I know well enough to quote over and over? It has been a struggle for me to memorize Scripture but how much effort have I really put into it? I will try and then get frustrated and then quit. Sound familiar? I am going to really try and make a whole hearted effort to memorize Scripture. We are not guaranteed that we will always have our Bibles to refer back to. I am almost certain we won't. It may not happen in our generation, but it will happen. Let's memorize God's Word so we will always have it in our hearts and on our lips.

Jim's comments:

The Word of God is something we can never fully know but I do study it on a daily basis. I have grown to love it and it is how I have come to know God intimately and to know His plan for me. As a believer there is no substitute for reading and studying the Bible. God communicates to us through His Word. He reveals Himself through it. He guides us, grows us, calms us, lifts us, prepares us, and so on and so forth. It is one of the four pillars of the Christian faith found in Acts 2:42.

Who Is Instructing You?

1 Timothy 1:5 But the goal of our instruction is love from a pure heart and a good conscience and a sincere faith.

Do you have access to a good Bible teacher? Someone who not only knows the Word but lives it. In 1 Timothy, Paul is instructing Timothy on how to handle false teachers who were mingling myths, genealogies, and keeping the law, with the Gospel. Paul stresses that the goal of teaching is love because that is what Christ is, God loving us first and sending Jesus to die so we might know real love.

Beware of teachers with an agenda or certain doctrines that they teach above all else. Watch to see if their teaching is to divide or unite. Is their teaching just to show off their knowledge or to help others put the Word into daily practice? Watch their walk, their talk, and most of all, their heart.

There also are teachers who have big hearts and push aside certain truths so as to be inclusive. They will not mention some verses or doctrines that may be damning to some they are teaching. They have a skewed view as to what is right and wrong and although they may be sincere, they are sincerely wrong.

Whoever is instructing you, it is your duty to check the Word yourself. A good Bible student is a good reader. There is no substitute for a good and godly Bible teacher, but in the end, you are responsible for what you believe. Who is instructing you?

Robbie's comments:

I have learned so much from my Sunday school teacher, Brian. He loves God's Word and loves to study it. He also loves teaching it to us. Do I agree with everything he teaches? No. He has interpreted some things differently than I have. We are never going to totally agree with others on everything. If we do agree totally with someone else, that usually means we are taking their word for it and not really studying it ourselves. Jim is another one that instructs me. He has taught me so much also. I am so thankful for those that are willing to teach and share their knowledge with others. They do have a gift of knowledge. However, it is still my responsibility to read and study the Bible myself to make sure what they are teaching is correct. That is why being in a good Bible study is so important. If we don't know God's Word, how can we live it or share it with others. Thank you Brian and Jim.

Jim's comments:

I have a multitude of good Bible teachers. Some are at my church, some on radio, some on T.V., and some write books. It is imperative to always check what others teach by going to the Word yourself and praying over the meaning. I also suggest several different translations and commentaries. Find a teacher that will challenge you and will allow you to question his interpretation. We learn so much by asking questions.

Are You Equipped?

2 Timothy 3:16-17 All Scripture is inspired by God and profitable for teaching, for reproof, for correction, for training in righteousness; so that the man of God may be adequate, equipped for every good work.

Are you thoroughly equipped for every good work? Can you correct someone? Can you reprimand another believer? Can you train anyone? Are you complete and competent? Are you well fitted as a Christian?

In this letter to Timothy, Paul is telling him how important the Word is in being a well equipped Christian. A good understanding of the Bible is necessary to know how to explain what we believe and why we believe it. 1 Peter 3:15 tells us to always be ready to give a good defense for the hope that is in us. Can you explain to someone why you believe what you believe? Or do you just say "the preacher said it and I believe it"? We must be prepared to give a good defense.

As you view your fellow brothers and sisters in Christ do you know enough of the Word to warn them when they begin to stray? Can you help keep them from hurting themselves or others? Do you have the confidence to correct someone before it's too late? Do you have that same confidence to help restore someone after they have strayed?

As believers we need to be able to speak freely and truthfully about what Christians should and should not be doing. We ought to do it out of love and with knowledge of the Word. We cannot afford to simply look the other way when we see others heading for disaster because we don't want to be uncomfortable by speaking the truth. We also cannot ignorantly sit by and watch lives destroyed because we don't know enough of the Truth. Knowing the Word is profitable in more ways than we can count.

Paul also says we need to know the Word so as to be equipped for every good work. We were saved from something and for something. If you haven't been taken home yet God has work for you here. We must not be just hearers of the Word but doers also. Remember we can do all things through Christ who strengthens us. Part of how He strengthens us is through knowing His Word.

We also need to be able to teach others. We don't necessarily have to teach a Bible study or a class, but in our everyday conversations can someone learn from us so as to help them stay the course? We teach through our actions as well as our words. Are you equipped?

Robbie's comment:

This is a hard one for me. I will be the first to admit that I do not know Scripture like I should or want to. I know concepts, stories and phrases but to actually be able to quote Scripture, book, chapter and verse, I fail miserably. I so take for granted the fact that I can just go get one of my many Bibles and search for Scripture. I can go to any room in my house and find at least a Bible or two. I need to think of what happens when I don't have a Bible to go get or pull up on the internet. I need to know Scripture. I want to know Scripture. I need to memorize it and have it engraved in my heart.

I am not very good at reprimanding and correcting other brothers and sisters either. I always feel like if I try to correct them they are going to think "who does she think she is to correct me?" It really shouldn't matter what they think. If they need correcting, I should be willing to do so in love. I'm not very good at that. I don't think any of us like to be corrected. Maybe that's part of it too. I don't like to be corrected so therefore, I don't like to correct others. It's just hard. But, if the correction is done in love then hopefully it will be received with love also. I can see I have some work to do today. I'd better get busy.

Jim's comments:

I believe that I am equipped. My problem is that sometimes I remain silent instead of confronting or I confront in a demeaning manner. I am trying to confront in love and also pray about what matters and what doesn't. Sometimes we worry too much about the small stuff and the big things slide right on by.

Are You Working Your Faith?

James 2:22 You see that faith was working with his works, and as a result of the works, faith was perfected.

Do you believe? Do you really believe? My pastor Mike asks this question when he is making a point about transferring what we believe into our actions. What he is basically saying is does your life reflect your beliefs? Does your faith have any works to prove it is real? Are you working your faith?

When it comes to your job, do you rely on your faith to get you ahead? Or, do you feel the need to take a few short cuts to speed up the process? Do you wait for the raise or go in and demand one? Do you have the faith to wait on God, to orchestrate the move up the ladder? At your job, when you are working your faith, you give your all, no matter what, even if you are passed over for that big promotion. Faith is knowing God is in control while we do the work.

Your faith is what transforms you so you can do good works. Works are not a substitute but a verification of salvation. When you are working your faith, you step out and do what God asks, without questions. Abraham was about to sacrifice his son, Isaac, because his faith led him to believe that God would bring him back to life (Hebrews 11:19). Faith caused the action (the attempted sacrifice). What actions has your faith caused in your life?

Unbelievers hear our talk, but more importantly, they watch our actions. They can tell if you really believe what you say. Our faith tells us to love our brothers. Do they see that? Our faith tells us to be cheerful givers. Do they see that? Our faith tells us our body is a temple. Do they see that? True faith transforms into actions that others can see. Are you working your faith?

Robbie's comments:

It is so true that you can tell more about a person from their actions then their words. We may truly believe something but if we aren't living it, it will be hard to convince others that we truly believe it. Jim and I stepped out in faith when we started this ministry. We basically cut our household income in half and must trust God that He will provide. It's His ministry and as long as we remain faithful, then He will bless it. I truly believe that and have to keep believing that when all the evidence tells me otherwise. I love the statement above that says "Faith is knowing God is in control while we do the work". It doesn't say while we just sit around and wait. We do our part and God will do His. It's a relationship. It's a covenant. We each have a role to play. Faith in action is what I strive for. I don't want people to have to ask about my faith. I want them to see me living it.

Jim's comments:

As I write this I am working my faith. I quit the best job I ever had to start a ministry not knowing where our income would come from or how much it would be. I only know after much prayer by me and others God said DO IT! Much like Gideon I still put the fleece out several times to be sure. I have known for about two years I would be in full time ministry but I envisioned a much different start. One with some financing first, but that's not stepping out in faith if I cover all the bases beforehand. It is as scary as it is exhilarating and I would not trade it for the world.

Are You Content?

Philippians 4:12 I know how to get along with humble means, and I also know how to live in prosperity; in any and every circumstance I have learned the secret of being filled and going hungry, both of having abundance and suffering need.

Contentment is the opposite of covetousness. It is exactly as Paul states above. To be satisfied in the present, whether hungry or filled. To be content is to realize that God is the Giver of all that is good. This does not mean it is wrong to desire more and better, but that desire should not come between you and the Father or compromise your walk.

Are you satisfied with your life as it stands today? Regardless of your outside circumstances, how do you feel inside? Are you doing all God desires you to do? Are you being all God desires you to be? Are you d.u.I? Remember, whether you are rich or poor, hungry or filled, your contentment comes from knowing who you are in Christ and your obedience to Him.

Beware of the dangers of confusing contentment with mediocrity. Many Christians squander away their lives because although they are saved from hell, they forgot they were also saved for something. This is just as bad as going through life placing your desire for more and better before your relationship with the Father. There is nothing wrong with more and better as long as God is first place in your life. We need rich, successful Christians so as to fund all the ministries it takes to build the Kingdom. Contentment comes from a growing relationship with the Father through Christ and obedience to His Word. Not only will you be content, He is likely to give you more and better. Are you content?

Robbie's comments:

If we were to be honest, I think we would all rather live in prosperity than poverty. It all boils down to giving God the glory no matter what we have or where we are in life. If you have been blessed with prosperity, then praise the Lord, giving Him thanks. I hope you are using that prosperity to bless others. That doesn't mean you have to give it all away. God wants to bless us as well. It's only when we put other things before Him that He becomes jealous. We have then crossed the line. God is the Giver of all that is good. We are never going to "arrive" at where we need to be in our walk with Him. We must walk daily with Him. We must talk daily with Him and we must thank Him daily for all that He has done and is going to do in our lives.

Jim's comments:

I am content most of the time. I do get impatient at times but I am getting much better. I am finally realizing God knows more about me and my goals than I do, and if I trust and obey Him, not only will I be content, but He will take me places I could never have imagined.

Who Are You Praying For?

1 Timothy 2:1-2 First of all, then, I urge that entreaties and prayers, petitions and thanksgivings, be made on behalf of all men, for kings and all who are in authority, so that we may lead a tranquil and quiet life in all godliness and dignity.

These verses make for quite a prayer list. Paul urges us to pray for all men because verse 4 clearly states that God desires all men to be saved. If each of us Christians would pray for all those around us, eventually it would cover "all men". Most of us are probably good at praying for family and close friends. It may be why Paul does not mention them here. It has been said, "Christians pray more to keep saints out of heaven, than to keep the lost out of hell." This means we pray more for those who we know are saved and dying and will be home with the Lord than those around us who we know are not saved.

Paul also urges us to pray for our leaders. This includes politicians, church leaders, community leaders, business leaders, teachers, police, military, etc. We must also pray for those leaders we disagree with. If everyone would pray for the leaders we now have, and pray for godly leaders to fill new vacancies, we could lead that tranquil and quiet life Paul is talking about. Prayer changes people, mostly the one praying.

Another good reason to pray for others is it takes the focus off of self – always a good thing. How are we to live a life of godliness and dignity unless we are praying regularly for others? Getting outside of self and asking for others to be blessed and know the truth is a sure way to bring about revival. Pray for others daily with all your heart and strength and I bet you will see a change around you, and especially in you. Who are you praying for?

Robbie's comments:

Jim gives me a list every morning on a sticky note of who we are praying for that day. We pray for one family member (or couple if they are married), one church family and then a different area of our lives that we change up monthly. It may be our finances, our ministry, our marriage, etc. I will put the sticky note on my desk at work where I can see it and every time I glance over at it I will pray for one or all of the people/things on the list. It's a great way to remind myself to pray for others. When we hear of things throughout the day or when people ask us to pray for them or about something going on in their lives, pray right then. I heard someone call them "pistol prayers". Shoot it up to God right away. If you are like me you have every intention of praying for these things but then forget. I shoot up pistol prayers all day long. Prayers don't have to be long and eloquent. They just need to be sincere. God knows our heart.

Jim's comments:

Because of my past I have developed a strong prayer life. It is because of Him of course and it is to glorify Him. I pray every morning through a long list and then continue to pray throughout the day. I keep a list of 5 in my pocket and pray over it all day. The list contains a family member, a church member, the theme for the month, and then two personal requests. Whenever I get frustrated or have to wait in line I pull out the list. If I am stuck in traffic, the list, feeling far from God, the list, close to God, the list, after awhile it becomes a habit. That is what it means to pray continuously.

How's Your Mama an 'em?

Ephesians 6:2 HONOR YOUR FATHER AND MOTHER (which is the first commandment with a promise).

How is your relationship with your parents? I know that it goes in stages. Stage one is when they are at our beck and call and just the slightest whimper can make a new mommy come running to the crib. Then, as we learn to walk and talk, we get a little defiant but still know who is in charge. After that, comes childhood where our parents are the smartest people in the world. Then comes the teen years where the old fogeys know absolutely nothing. When we become an adult we see them as our equals. Once we have children, and are parents ourselves, we realize how truly great they were and are. Not everyone goes through this cycle and some parents are abusive, both physically and verbally. I am truly sorry for those of you who had parents like that, but the Word says to honor your mother and father with no qualifiers. Remember this is the first commandment with a promise.

If your relationship with either of your parents is not what it should be, I pray you would do your part to try and make it so. Some relationships can't be repaired but God will bless you if you do your part, regardless if they do theirs.

If your relationship is on good terms, continue to let them know you love and respect them. Ask for their advice and honor their judgment. Tell them often how great of a job they did raising you. Pray for them and with them. How's your mama an 'em?

Robbie's comments:

I am so thankful to have such wonderful parents. I don't say that lightly. I tell them all the time how much I love them and am thankful for them. I am blessed. I can only say and I truly believe that all parents just do the best they can. Their intent is not to hurt. We are selfish by nature and sometimes parents never outgrow their selfish desires. They put their own desires before their children and this is transferred from generation to generation. My prayer for you is that if there needs to be healing between you and your parents you will take care of that before it is too late. Make the first move. It may not be easy but there is peace on the other side. Even if they don't respond how you think they should (and they probably won't), you will know that you made the effort, you did your part and you can move on with no regrets. Continue to pray for them and be at peace that you have done your part.

Jim's comments:

This is one I am not good at. I moved from home when I was 22 and have been gone 27 years. Most of that time I have been addicted to something and all my relationships have suffered, especially the long distant ones. I am working on it and will do better.

What's In Your Billfold?

1Timothy 6:17-18 Instruct those who are rich in this present world not to be conceited or to fix their hope on the uncertainty of riches, but on God, who richly supplies us with all things to enjoy. Instruct them to do good, to be rich in good works, to be generous and ready to share.

Ah, the evil rich, despised by some, distrusted by others, hounded by most all for donations. This country and its free market economy used to celebrate people who risked it all to start a business with the small possibility of becoming prosperous. Now they are chastised for not giving their fair share in taxes or they don't spend it the way "others" think they should. Truth be known, most of the rich in this country are hard working people who have persevered after failing. Politicians talk of three classes of people, the poor, the working class, and the rich, like the rich don't work. Let's look at what Paul tells Timothy about the believers who are rich.

The first thing he says is not to have too high an opinion of themselves or to fix their hope on their wealth. Riches do not save them and they are a blessing from God. God gives us riches to enjoy and to do good with. We cannot let what is in our wallet define us. We need to always look at it as a tool God has given us to use for the Kingdom. Some may have received a special ability or talent with which to further the Kingdom. The ability to make money should be treated the same way. He also tells them to be generous and always ready to share. Remember you cannot out give God.

If you happen to be wealthy I applaud you, but be careful not to trust in your riches. Mark 10:25 eludes to the fact that it is hard for a rich man to trust in Christ and not his own wealth, but it could also be said it is easier for a poor man to trust Him because they have little else. Either way, trust Christ and let Him define you, not what is in your wallet. What's in your billfold?

Robbie's comments:

Money is such a funny animal. I, for one, like it. One of the things I get great pleasure from is being able to pay my bills on time. I didn't say we are at the point financially where this occurs every month but we are getting closer and closer. When Jim was full into his addiction we struggled with money all the time. I couldn't trust him with it. He would lie about how much he made and how much he spent. He would get fired from jobs and not tell me and say he was looking for another job but wasn't. He had been known to forge my name on checks to cash. We got months behind in all of our bills to the point of having our home foreclosed. It has taken over three years to finally start seeing the light of day. Of course in the midst of all that we sent two of our daughters, Casey and Corrie, to college and recently helped Corrie pay for a wedding. I say all that to say that I am not the least bit jealous of those that have wealth and riches. My prayer is that someday God will bless Jim and me with enough wealth to help many others. There is not a day that goes by that I don't hear of some cause, some family or some organization that I say to myself "I wish I had the money to help them". If we only want to have enough to get by and pay our bills then that is probably all we are ever going to have. I want enough to give to others. I want to bless others and give God all the praise and glory. Right now, there's not much in my wallet but hopefully one day soon there will be an abundance that I can share with many.

Jim's comments:

When I was younger and totally lost, I used to judge others by how much money they made and judge myself the same way. Now as a believer, I have a much better understanding of money and people. I no longer judge people by what they make. I do understand the importance of money and its use in the Kingdom and place it in the proper perspective.

What's Your Armor?

Ephesians 6:13-17 Therefore, take up the full armor of God, so that you will be able to resist in the evil day, and having done everything, to stand firm. Stand firm therefore, having girded your loins with truth, and having put on the breastplate of righteousness, and having shod your feet with the preparation of the Gospel of Peace; in addition to all, taking up the shield of faith with which you will be able to extinguish all the flaming arrows of the evil one. And take The Helmet of Salvation, and the sword of the Spirit, which is the word of God.

If every believer would put on this armor every morning as soon as their feet hit the floor what power the church would have. People would actually see a difference in us starting with our own families. We would be truthful and our hearts would be loving. We would bring peace and we would not worry over remarks from others. We would know we were covered by the blood of salvation and we have the Word of God to stand on. The world could not stand in our way.

First off, we would have to gird our loins with the truth. To gird your loins meant to secure the lower part of your back. This was to prevent an attack from behind. When we protect ourselves by living in truth we needn't worry about the hits that come from behind. Gossip, slander, and rumor have little effect on someone whose life is lived openly in truth for all to see. False accusations cannot be substantiated.

Next is the breastplate which protects the heart. Our breastplate of righteousness protects our heart in two ways. The first is from God's wrath. When God looks at us He sees Jesus' righteousness not our fallen sinful state. Second is from Satan's accusations. When Satan accuses us, Jesus stands in our place and we are acquitted. This keeps our heart free from any guilt. We are declared righteous which allows us to use our heart to love others as He loves us. We cannot be condemned by our past and now can live boldly in a state of forgiveness.

Just as a good soldier today knows the importance of proper footwear it was more so in Biblical times. There weren't very many Jeeps or Hum-Vees to ride around in. They had to march everywhere they went. The opposing army knew this and would plant gaul-traps and sharp sticks to obstruct the advancing army. We, as Christians, are to be shod with the preparation of the Gospel of Peace. We must be firm footed enough in our faith to be ready to share it with anyone at the prompting of the Holy Spirit. We must also be ready to give a good defense of our hope in the Gospel for those who lay traps and snares for us. We have the peace that surpasses all understanding and must be ready to share it whenever and wherever.

The shield was used to protect you from arrows and swords. Your shield of faith will protect you from Satan's arrows of deception and guilt. If you use your faith and stand on God's Word and promises no matter what the world, Satan, or your flesh tell you, you will be victorious. One of Satan's most powerful tools is to get us to doubt. Then he can distract and then deceive. When faith walks in, fear walks out. We know how the story ends.

The helmet protected the soldier's head. Everyone knows how fatal a head wound can be. Our helmet of salvation assures us that our spirit cannot be fatally injured. We should not fear death because we know what is on the other side. The helmet of salvation assures us we will never again be separated from God. That is a good "helmet law".

The sword is an offensive as well as defensive weapon. The sword of the Spirit, which is the Word of God, is also an offensive as well as defensive weapon. It can be used offensively to bring people to Christ and defensively to ward off Satan's attack just as Jesus did in Matthew 4. When Satan tried to tempt Him, Jesus quoted Scripture. No matter what's going on in your life there is a Scripture to lift you up or to correct you and get you back on track. To use the sword effectively you have to know it. Sharpen that sword everyday by studying and then living it. What's your armor?

Robbie's comments:

For me there are two basics to living the Christian life. One is to walk daily under the influence of the Holy Spirit; living Acts 2:42. That is what this book is all about, how to live and walk daily. It is learned behavior that comes with time and discipline. The other basic for me is to make sure that all my armor gets put on every day. This is also a learned behavior that comes with time and discipline. This chapter was like finding a treasure. I could see the visual. I could see the belt, the helmet, the shield, the sword, the breastplate. It all made sense to me. Each piece had its own purpose and they were all for my protection. The problem was I wasn't wearing most of them. I still forget to put ALL of my armor on daily. When I think of knowing God's Word as a sword, as a weapon, it takes on a whole new meaning. It is not only to comfort me and teach me, it is to protect me and defend me. When I feel the world is heavy or I start to doubt, have I forgotten to put on my shield of faith? We must go out fully armed and fully armored. Read this scripture again and remember each day when you get dressed to put on the full armor of God.

Jim's comments:

This is a tough one to do all the time. It is a lifelong battle and we need to be putting the armor on daily but life tends to get in the way. That is why we need to be d.u.I. Daily putting on the armor because Satan is always looking for the day we are unprepared so he can attack and do the most damage.

Conclusion

Well, how did you do? Did you get them all right? Just kidding! We hope you at the very least know the Holy One of God. Again, we would like to state the questions are for you to delve into your walk to see where you stand. They are not for pride issues to say look at me I'm doing it right, or to guilt you into the proper behavior. We just want Christians to have an effective walk so we can make a difference in the world.

To be effective we have to know the Word, have a good instructor, and be equipped so we can work out our faith. Our contentment or lack thereof will show the world if we truly believe what we say about our God supplying all our needs. Praying for others, how we treat our parents, and what we do with our money speaks volumes to others about our faith. And if we try to go through the day without our armor we are just asking to be attacked. Once attacked without our armor we have no defense and surly we will stumble and weaken our effectiveness and our testimony. So let's tackle ten more questions and start working out our faith.

Chapter Two

Let's Tackle Ten More!

Do You Know The Way?

John 14:5-6 Thomas said to Him, "Lord, we do not know where You are going, how do we know the way?" Jesus said to him, "I am the way, and the truth, and the life; no one comes to the Father but through Me".

Up or down? Which way are you going? In these verses we see that Jesus did not come to show us the way, but rather He is the way. In the previous chapter, Jesus tells the disciples, in veiled statements, about his future betrayal, death, and resurrection. He doesn't talk about being crucified, he talks of being glorified. He also tells them that He is going away to prepare a place for them. They, still looking for the earthly kingdom, think Jesus is going to a physical place to begin that kingdom. Thomas, in essence is saying, "Look, we do not know where you are going so how can we get there"?

Now, on this side of the cross, we know what Jesus was talking about. The Way is the belief in Him. Eternal life is the belief in Him. Truth is the belief in Him. Access to the Father is belief in Him. That is why the early church was called The Way. (Acts 9:2, 19:9).

Are you still looking for direction? If you died today, would you be in the place that Jesus has gone ahead to prepare? Do you know the Way?

Robbie's comments:

It is somewhat comforting to know that the disciples were also confused at times! They didn't always understand and perhaps sometimes had that deer in the headlight look also. There are so many people and religions out there that believe that there are many ways to God. I know some who claim to be Christians who are not convinced of the fact that there is only one way to God and that is through a relationship with Jesus. Perhaps you are one of those or know of someone who is. The Bible is very clear that there is only one way to God and that is through His Son. "No one comes to the Father but through me (Jesus)". That is why it is so important to know what the Bible says and teaches. Read it and then get around other brothers and sisters that you trust and respect and discuss it. I can read it all day long but it is only when I get around other believers and discuss it in depth does the clarity of it all start taking place for me.

Jim's comment:

I do know the Way and I am so glad I do. My life will never be the same since I started following Christ. My prayer is that anyone reading this would be SURE they know the Way also. We also need to be sure He is our Lord and not just our free ticket out of hell.

Does Your Church Preach The Bible?

1 Timothy 4:13 Until I come, give attention to the public reading of Scripture, to exhortation and teaching.

When you are in church on Sundays do you get a good dose of Biblical truth, or a social commentary? Current events and trends, or verses to encourage? The need to be good, or the need for a Savior?

Here Paul is telling Timothy to publically read the Word so as to encourage as well as teach his members. Timothy had to combat Gnosticism which was seeping into the Christian faith. Gnostics claim to have a special "knowledge" and live in an elevated "spiritual" existence. Paul's message was to counter the lies with the truth of Scripture. That is exactly what we need today to counter New Age Mysticism, cults, and "special" insights into the Christian faith.

We, as humans, are apt to forget and slow to remember the goodness of God. Just look to the Old Testament to see time and time again how God's people forgot and drifted towards idol worship. We also need to know what to do and what not to do as followers of Christ. The Bible is our instruction manual. It is also very, very deep and a good pastor can help give us the full meaning of the Word and how to apply it to our everyday lives so that it actually accomplishes something.

Last, but not least, the reason the Bible should be preached every Sunday is that all those attending are not saved. If the lost can't find the salvation message in church, then where will they find it? Does your church preach the Bible?

Robbie's comments:

I attend and serve at a very strong Bible believing and preaching church. It is very important that the church you attend is grounded in God's Word and truths. Our pastor is always reading and preaching from God's Word. He challenges us to not just take his word for it but to look it up and read it for ourselves. We are never going to find a church that believes 100% the same way we do. There are minor issues that in the scheme of things don't matter and could be debated from now until eternity. They are not eternal issues and we shouldn't get caught up in them and waste too much time debating them. As long as we agree on the salvation issue (there is only one way to God and eternity with Him and that is through a relationship with Christ), we can agree to disagree on the other things. If you are not in a good, Bible believing, teaching, and preaching church, please start your journey THIS week in finding one. It is so important to keeping your walk with God in balance. You will see.

Jim's comments:

Good sound Bible teaching is one of the essentials for a rock solid church. I have been to churches where the Bible is hardly mentioned. Robert, a friend of mine, went to visit a church where the pastor actually apologized for having too many Scripture references and I think it may have been five at the most. We do not need social commentary, personal opinions, or new age philosophy from the pulpit. We need solid Bible teaching to equip us for the task at hand.

Who Are You Hanging With?

1 Corinthians 15:33 Do not be deceived: "Bad company corrupts good morals."

The Greek word, phtheiro¯, and its English counterpart, corrupt, are almost identical in definition. The Greek means "to spoil by any process" while the English definition is "cause to become rotten or bad, change in any degree from good to bad." Paul is strongly stating that who you associate with is of great importance. It's almost as if two people are hanging out - the law of gravity will bring the good one down to the level of the bad one.

Obviously, we have to be around the lost to spread the Gospel. Not all the lost are bad company. Sometimes Christians can even be bad company with their sour attitude and negative outlook. What we are talking about is forming relationships with people who can influence us in a negative way. Remember, to corrupt is to change in any degree from good to bad. Those little degrees of change over time can lead us far from God's direction for our life.

We also need to be around the lost and mediocre Christians to let our light shine as an example of how the abundant life is to be lived. The key here is for you to be the influence. Do not be deceived. In all relationships someone is being influenced. Who are you hanging with?

Robbie's comments:

I can't stand drama and whiners. I struggle with people who make excuses for everything. I like to hang around people who are serious about their Christian walk and want to keep moving forward. They desire to learn and grow and are "on fire for Jesus"! The problem is I have a hard time finding these people. I have a lot of friends who are fun to be with and we have a good time and I am thankful for them but I am at a season in my life where I want to go deep. The deeper I go, the deeper I want to go. Jim and I had a couple over at our house last weekend that we hadn't seen in a while and she said to me that she is tired of people who are stuck and not excited about Jesus. I can say that I was stuck for many years. I never walked away from my faith but I wasn't putting very much effort into it either. As a result, I was not full of much joy or peace. There came a point in my life when I realized that God does not fulfill His end of His promises until we have done our end first. When I started reading the promises of God they are almost always tied to something we must do first. He rewards our faith and obedience; He doesn't just give us handouts. As you read your Bible today and the rest of this week, try to recognize all the things we are to do or say in order to receive the blessings from God. It was very eye opening to me. I pray it is for you as well.

Jim's comments:

My best suggestion for this is, if you can't be the one doing the influencing, and their behavior is corrupting you, then I would be gone. We, as humans, can only stand so much temptation, and to place ourselves where we are doing no good, and can actually be influenced for evil, makes no sense. Be aware of what's going on and be careful of that slow fade.

Do You Walk In His Commandments?

2 John 1:6 And this is love, that we walk according to His commandments. This is the commandment, just as you have heard from the beginning, that you should walk in it.

Walk in love. Sometimes this is a difficult task. The pressures of life, the fast pace of our society, having to deal with offensive people, and sometimes even having to deal with our brothers and sisters in Christ makes this difficult. As Christians, we are to be different from the rest. We are set apart. So, how do we walk in love?

Paul gives us the example of how to love in 1 Corinthians 13. We are to be patient with others. We are not to be jealous of what God has blessed others with, or to brag about how He has blessed us. We are not to act selfish, rude, or hold resentments. We were forgiven so we must forgive. We are to rejoice in the truth. We are to bear each other's burdens. We are to endure all things and most of all, find hope in all things. We must yield to the Spirit and not to the flesh in all of our relationships.

We can not afford to miss the mark on this one. The world is watching. Could your life be put on trial and there be enough evidence to convict you of being daily under His influence? Do you walk in His commandments?

Robbie's comments:

All I can say here is that I am a work in progress. I am trying to live daily under the Influence of the Holy Spirit. I am definitely more aware of my words and actions. My prayer life has taken on a whole new dimension. I'm reading my Bible more and asking God to reveal Himself to me like never before. They are not just words on a page anymore. They have taken on meaning in my life. I'm reading Scripture I have read many times before and all of a sudden, I get it! I understand it, it makes sense. It's like the light bulb is going off! I have brothers and sisters in Christ that I call my good friends that I never had before. My priorities have changed and my heart has changed and continues to change. I'm by no means anywhere close to where I need to be but I am aware of that and continuing to work on it.

Jim's comments:

For me trying to walk in love takes determination, prayer, and a whole lot of grace. I am trying to get better, but old habits die hard. I used to not care for people. Then I started to just tolerate them. After awhile I actually started to like people. I can say that I am better at it today than I was yesterday and with His help I will be even better at it tomorrow.

Do You Accept Those Weak In Faith?

Romans 14:1 Now accept the one who is weak in faith, but not for the purpose of passing judgment on his opinions.

When we talk about those weak in faith we are basically talking about maturity. We are not talking about length, but of depth. Not how long you have been a Christian, but how deep is your relationship with the Father. It is about how much of your day is controlled by the Holy Spirit and how much is lived in the flesh. It is about being d.u.I.

When Paul wrote this chapter, the problems then were what foods people ate and what days were holy. Some Christians wanted to keep the clean and unclean meat rules while some were keeping the Jewish holidays. The Word is clear on both of these issues. That does not give us permission to chastise or judge those who want to keep them because they do not have a full sense of their liberty in Christ. Those that do must demonstrate this liberty by being sensitive to others and loving them where they are. We must also be careful of adding manmade rules to make ourselves appear holy.

God's Word gives us acceptable and unacceptable behavior. I find nothing wrong with Christians having a drink. The Word says do not get drunk. We should not use this liberty when we are around recovering alcoholics, as we would not want to cause a brother to stumble. Each one of us is accountable to God for our actions. Liberty must be united with love for others.

Those weak in faith need a loving, mature Christian to come along side of them and help them deepen their walk. They need guidance, not talking behind their backs. They need prayer, not judgment. And we all need love. Do you accept those weak in faith?

Robbie's comments:

If you are weak in faith because you have not been a Christian for very long then you are starting an amazing journey. If you have been a Christian for a while but are weak in faith, it is never too late to get back on track. Either way, I would encourage you to find a mature Christian (of the same sex) that you respect and ask them if perhaps they would spend some time with you. Get to know each other and start walking together. We have a mentoring program at my church and the first time you go through the program you have to be a mentee. My mentor was the pastor's wife, Judy. What an incredibly awesome time we spent together. She was a gift from God. God blessed me so much through her and He knew exactly what I needed. I was ashamed to let people know about Jim and what a mess our lives were. I was wearing the mask and trying to minimize the hurt and anger I was feeling. I needed someone who was strong in their faith that would encourage me and she did just that. No matter where we are in our walk, we need to be hanging around those that are more mature and can challenge us to reach that next level.

Jim's comments:

It is hard for guys to accept weakness, period. We keep our weaknesses hidden from everybody and don't tolerate it much in others. My disdain for mediocrity is why we wrote this book and started a ministry. I just need to learn how to help others with love. Being gentle and trying to come along side, not pull or push them kicking and screaming all the way.

Are You Anxious?

Matthew 6:34 (Amplified) So do not worry or be anxious about tomorrow, for tomorrow will have worries and anxieties of its own. Sufficient for each day is its own trouble.

Are you anxious? Do you have an uneasy feeling about what will happen tomorrow? Do you feel the need to know what's coming up next in your life? What keeps you awake at night? Are they legitimate concerns or just plain worries? Are you so busy worrying about tomorrow that you can't enjoy today? Let's look at what Jesus says about worry.

In verse 25 Jesus takes it a step further. He says "Do not be worried about your life", not just tomorrow. He wants you focused on Him today, not what might happen tomorrow. Satan wants us focused on what might be, so we can't do what we ought to, which is Kingdom work. One of Satan's best tools is to keep us paralyzed with worry over tomorrow so we can't live for Christ today. We need to remember the A.A. slogan "One day at a time".

We can achieve this peace of living daily for Christ by starting our day off with Him. Give God the first part of your day by praying and reading His Word. Focus on how He would have you serve Him that day. Pray often throughout the day and listen closely for the Holy Spirit to speak to you. When worries do enter your mind, pray and turn them over to Him. Write down Scripture verses to read during the day to keep your mind on God. Remember, it's okay to plan for the future just don't stress over it. Start off your day with Him and let Him carry you from there. Live each day like He's coming back tonight. Are you anxious?

Robbie's comments:

I just got through listening to a song called "One Pair of Hands". It was talking about Jesus and how one pair of hands healed, fed thousands and raised the dead. Whatever we are going through, His one pair of Hands can hold it and handle it. I have to admit that I do find myself getting anxious about things. For me, it's progress, not perfection. I am anxious about finding the financial supporters and investors to get this book published. I am anxious about my daughter finding a job. I try not to dwell on the things that I have no control over. I don't dwell on things near what I used to. I am quicker about turning them over to God and trusting that He will take care of them. I can honestly, and without a doubt, say that I could not do that or come this far without maturing in my relationship with God. By growing in Christ, we grow in every area of our lives. We think differently and act differently. The more we mature the more like Christ we become and the less we will worry and be anxious. My days are more peaceful and focused on Him when I start them out focused on Him. God loves us and does not want to see us worried or anxious. Turn it over to Him. He wants us to depend on Him.

Jim's comments:

Most of my anxiety comes on the way to the golf course. I love to play and can't wait to get there. Some days the way I play I can't wait to leave the course. Mostly in life I have learned to not get anxious. I have to continually remember Who is in charge and trust Him. I am learning to let go and let God and it has turned out to be an awesome ride!

How Long Have You Knocked?

Matthew 7:7 (Amplified) Keep on asking and it will be given you; keep on seeking and you will find; keep on knocking [reverently] and [the door] will be opened to you.

The reason I used the Amplified here is that it comes closest to the actual Greek. The Greek means to continue to ask, seek and knock. Not just once, but continually. I believe a lot of prayers go unanswered because of a lack of persistence. God wants to see if we really want what we ask for, or are we just throwing out empty words?

When you are praying for something your heart truly desires and you continue no matter what, one of three things will happen. He will change your heart, say "not now", or you will receive it!

If you ask for something with the wrong motives, James 4:3 tells us you will not receive it. This will require a change of heart because God does not answer the prayers of the flesh. He will give you what your heart truly desires when it is prayed for through the Spirit.

He may say, "Not now". Your heart's desire has not changed and He clearly hasn't told you "no". Now is the time to persevere; to continue to ask, seek and knock. How many pray for salvation for a loved one and then give up after a week? Possibly, you have to be prepared to be able to accept what you are praying for and preparation takes time.

The third possibility is that you get what you pray for. Your heart and motives were right, you were properly prepared and He knows you will use it for the good of the Kingdom.

You must continue asking, seeking, and knocking regardless of what others think or say. Do not be afraid to pray big prayers that your heart truly desires. Just continue to ask, seek and knock. How long have you knocked?

Robbie's comments:

I remember praying for Jim's sobriety and not that he would just quit drinking and using but that God would make him whole

53

again. I knew that it was not God's will for Jim to be an alcoholic and addict and doing all the things he was doing. Therefore, I knew my prayers lined up with God's will. I just had to persevere and keep praying. It was hard. It was probably the hardest thing I have ever been through. But I was not going to give up. I had no idea what the timing would be and of course it was not quick enough for me. Everyone wondered why I was still with Jim and why I didn't leave him or kick him out. They would have understood if I had, but then I would have given up and God was not telling me to give up. He wanted to see just how serious I was, just how long I would keep seeking Him, just how long I would ask and keep asking. Nobody said it would be easy to seek and keep seeking, ask and keep asking, knock and keep knocking, but oh how worth it when we get to the other side and see the miracles that God is not only capable of, but desires to show us.

Jim's comments:

Prayer is my favorite subject. I will persistently knock, ask, and seek until He answers. I want to be sure that everything I do is His will so I will hound Him until He answers. I believe that is what He desires of us; that continued reliance on Him for everything.

Do You Love Your Children?

Ephesians 6:4 Fathers, do not provoke your children to anger, but bring them up in the discipline and instruction of the Lord.

This message is for both parents. I believe the reason it reads "fathers" is that mothers have that built in nurturing personality and fathers have the discipline and protection role. In carrying out this discipline and protection fathers can be demanding, overbearing, and impatient. Fathers haven't changed much since Paul's time.

Paul is telling parents not to be harsh or degrading in speech. Children's self-esteem can be shattered in one sentence in an angry tone that is not justified. Fathers should not discipline their children for accidentally spilling milk. Making a mess is what children do. When they look at you with a smirk and deliberately turn the glass upside down, it's go time. When they don't live up to your expectations, it's time to encourage, not berate. When they make mistakes, correct them and guide them back on track. Laugh with them, pray with them, play with them, hug them and above all else, be the example.

The second part of this verse is about educating them. That is the parent's responsibility, not the schools. Parents should know what is being taught at school and making sure it does not undermine their teaching at home. They need to be sure they are learning. The parents are to teach them God's Word. The father is the spiritual head of the house and must know the Word himself to impart it to his children. He must also live it and be the example of Christ. Do you love your children?

Robbie's comments:

I believe one of the best gifts you can give your children is self-confidence. This is done by years of building them up and not tearing them down. Encourage them and love them enough to say "no" at times. It is more important to be their parent than their friend. Know who your children's friends are, know who their parents are, know

55

what they are looking at on the computer, know where they are at all times. I think children want to know their parents care enough to hold them to some ground rules.

I was at a high school basketball game last week and saw a 6 or 7 year old boy just roaming around. He opened the door to the gym and went outside. I went out and told him he needed to come inside and he said he didn't want to, he wanted to play outside. I asked him where his mom and dad were and he said they were working. I asked who he was there with and he said his brother. Of course, his brother was nowhere to be found and this little boy was just left on his own to do whatever he wanted to do. I made him come inside but it broke my heart. Kids need structure and rules and of course love. I do love my children and if you have children, I know you love yours too. I truly believe we all do the best we can. They don't come with instruction books. However, if we are grounded in God's instruction book, it makes it easier. Go love on your kids today!

Jim's comment:

I most definitely love my children, but I am sure I do not show it all the time. Because of my past I have not always been there for them and I know I have let them down many, many times. I am trying to make up for the past and I now have a wonderful relationship with all of my children. I wish I hadn't wasted all that time but I can't go back so all I can do is move forward and love them to the best of my ability with the help of Christ.

Do You Want To Prosper In Every Way?

3 John 2 (Amplified) Beloved, I pray that you may prosper in every way and [that your body] may keep well, even as [I know] your soul keeps well and prospers.

John is writing this letter to Gaius, a beloved brother in Christ. John prays for him to prosper in every way. Is this John's desire for Gaius only? Did God include this letter in the Bible because He desires us to prosper? What does it mean to prosper?

Both the Greek word and the English word for prosper have the same meaning. The meaning is to be successful, thrive, succeed in reaching, or succeed in business affairs; it doesn't necessarily mean money. To be successful is to achieve one's sought after goals. It *can* be money. The chances are if you are successful at something, the money will follow.

As we read the rest of this letter, we will see the plan to prosper in every way. He is walking in the Truth (vs.3, 4) and acting faithfully (vs.5). Others have heard of his love (vs.6) and he is imitating good (vs.11). If we apply all the above principles to our lives, combined with much prayer and using our gifts, we will prosper in every way. God desires us to be successful at whatever we do. God is not pleased with mediocrity and neither should we. Do you want to prosper in every way?

Robbie's comments:

I don't know about you but I sure want to prosper in every way. I hope you do too. When we hear the word "prosper" we automatically think of money, but when we hear "in every way" we realize it means so much more. I think as Christians we fail to realize how much God wants us to prosper in every way. The world and even sometimes other believers make it sound like there is something wrong with wanting to prosper. We have to remember we are royalty, heirs with Christ, princes and princesses. He wants us to be all that He has made us to be and have all that He has for us. I hope you will remember today that God does want you to prosper. He wants you to succeed. He wants you to walk in His truth and act faithfully. Every way means every way, financially, physically, emotionally and spiritually, etc. By walking daily under His Influence, we start to experience that prosperity.

Jim's comments:

I believe we should try to be successful in everything we do. All that Christ has done for us demands that we do our best. It bothers me to see Christians not living up to their potential and then making excuses for it. If He has not taken you home yet He has a plan for you and wants it done with the best you have to offer. God certainly gave the best He had to offer for you and me, namely Christ. I don't know what it means to you to prosper in every way. I know we are all different and success means different things to different people, but if we do our best at everything we do, we will prosper in every way.

Are You A Good Christian Soldier?

2 Timothy 2:4 No soldier in active service entangles himself in the affairs of everyday life, so that he may please the one who enlisted him as a soldier.

One thing a soldier will learn in basic training is his place in the chain of command. He will also learn to take orders with no questions asked. They will teach him to be in shape, disciplined, and to rely on his fellow soldiers. He will be reminded again and again how submission to those in authority is absolutely critical on the battlefield. He will learn it is an honor and duty to serve and protect his country. How does his service stack up against your Christian service?

Have you learned the chain of command that God is in charge and not you? Do you take orders well when the Holy Spirit speaks to you? Are you in spiritual shape by being daily in the Word, praying often, fellowshipping with other believers, and attending and serving in a local church? Is your life disciplined so as to remove the unwanted behaviors and activities that hinder your walk? Do you rely on the counsel of other believers? Just as Jesus was under submission to the Father, even to the point of death, are you willing to die for your faith? Are you pleasing the One who enlisted you as a soldier?

Make no mistake, we are soldiers and the battle is real. There is one difference though; we fight FROM victory not for victory. Death has been defeated but that does not make the evil one powerless. We must be a good Christian soldier and use all of our armor to defeat the effects of the world, Satan and the flesh. The battle will end one day and we are assured victory and we have the best retirement plan there is. So be a good soldier and don't entangle yourself with worldly concerns, don't let Satan deceive you, and keep your flesh in check. Are you a good Christian soldier?

Robbie's comments:

Ok, well if I go by what a good soldier is from above, my answer would have to be "no". I am not in shape, I am not very disciplined and I have problems relying on others because usually they let me down. The one thing I do understand is the battle is real. Ephesians 6 tells me to put on the full armor of God so I can take my stand against the devil's schemes. When I have been blindsided by the world or the enemy I ask myself "What piece or pieces or my armor did I forget to put on today?" If you are not aware that you are to put on your armor each and every day go to Ephesians 6 and read this chapter. I love the visual of actually walking around wearing these pieces of armor. The enemy can not attack me if I am armored up! It will help you prepare for battle so that you can be a good Christian soldier.

Jim's comments:

Being a good Christian soldier is a lifelong journey. The key is not to go A.W.O.L. Again it falls under being d.u.I. Daily doing what God desires of us, daily preparing for the battle, daily helping our brothers and showing others the love of Christ. I am lucky the Holy Spirit is not like a drill sergeant or my eardrums would be busted by now.

Conclusion

Are you certain about where you will spend eternity? Up or down? There is assurance if you know the Way. That is why a good church that preaches truth is so important. Knowing truth helps keep you from being anxious and guides you to walk in His commandments. A good church trains you as a soldier to help those weak in the faith. It will enable you to be the one doing the influencing. It will show you God's love so you can in turn love your children, but your church is just the starting point. It is a place to connect, refresh, worship, learn, and start to serve. Then we take all that out into the world. That is how we will be different.

Prayer and a few other topics will come up more than once in these 101 questions. Repetition is used for a reason, it means something is important. Prayer is one of the Christians most under-utilized tools. Billy Graham says "To get a nation back on its feet, we must first get on our knees". J Sidlow Baxter says "Men may spurn our appeals, reject our message, oppose our arguments, despise our person, but they are helpless against our prayers". How long are you willing to knock? Show God you truly desire fellowship with Him by talking to Him and taking everything to Him in prayer. If you truly desire to prosper in every way you need Him. Take time to pray right now that God would open your heart and mind to what He would have you receive from these questions.

Chapter Three

Got Your Heart And Mind Open?

Who Is Your Priest?

Hebrews 7:26-27 For it was fitting for us to have such a high priest, holy, innocent, undefiled, separated from sinners and exalted above the heavens; who does not need daily, like those high priests, to offer up sacrifices, first for His own sins and then for the sins of the people, because this He did once for all when He offered up Himself.

Do you have a priest? Do you need a priest? The Israelites' sacrificial system was operated by the priests who were descendants of Aaron. There were four main types of sacrifice. The burnt offering was originally made to atone for sin, but later had an element of thanksgiving. The cereal offering was also for forgiveness of sins. The peace offering and thank offering were associated with forgiveness of sins and were often followed by a fellowship meal. The fourth type of sacrificial offering was the guilt and sin offering. This offering was for ceremonial defilement. Wheeww! Thank God for grace!

Although the priest would oversee the sacrifices, he himself would have to offer up a sacrifice for his sins in order to be clean enough to offer up the people's sacrifices. This proves the fact that whoever desires to come into God's presence must first be clean and forgiven of sins.

Thanks to Jesus, we have that One High Priest who does not have to make atonement for Himself first. He is our atonement. He tore the veil to the Holy of Holies. We can now enter into fellowship with the Father. So remember, Jesus is the only priest who can forgive sins and He is that mediator between us and the Father. Be careful of any religion that puts anyone or anything between you and Christ, the one and only High Priest. Who is your priest?

Robbie's comments:

Let me be very clear here that there is nothing Biblical about confessing your sins to a priest. Jesus came so that we could have full access to God the Father through Christ's death, burial and resurrection. The veil was a separator. It has now been torn. I think the concept of a priest is one of those things that is taught and never questioned. We must not be paralyzed in our walk by formalities and traditions that have no Biblical basis. My pastor is just a man that God has put in that leadership position. He has no magical power or authority. We must be careful who we render power and authority to in our lives.

Jim's comments:

My Priest is Jesus Christ. The one and only Priest we will ever need. He did it all and when He was done He said "It is finished".

Where Is Your Foundation?

Luke 6:47-49 Everyone who comes to Me and hears My words and acts on them, I will show you whom he is like: he is like a man building a house, who dug deep and laid a foundation on the rock; and when a flood occurred, the torrent burst against that house and could not shake it, because it had been well built. But the one who has heard and has not acted accordingly, is like a man who built a house on the ground without any foundation; and the torrent burst against it and immediately it collapsed, and the ruin of that house was great.

Is your foundation just on the surface or dug deep into the rock? Jesus clearly states in this parable, not only do you have to know His Word, but you have to live out His Word to have a firm foundation. One of the problems in Christianity today is not acting on what we know to be true. We are sometimes too timid to act, or we procrastinate, or just plain disobey. You can study the Word until Christ returns, but if you fail to live it out in your daily life, what good is it? If you act no different than the world, what do you have to offer them?

In verse 48 Jesus says, "The man dug deep". Here He is simply saying that it will require work. The man did not dig just below the surface but rather down deep into the rock. It requires discipline to be an effective Christian. You have to be in the Word daily, even when you don't feel like it. You have to pray often throughout the day. You have to fellowship with other believers. You have to belong and serve in a local church. You have to yield to the Holy Spirit. All this requires effort. That is digging deep!

The reward of doing the work and digging deep and having a solid foundation is that you will be different from the world. It will be easier to deal with the world around you, easier to overcome the desires of the flesh, and harder to be deceived by Satan. If you do not do the work required you will be like the man who built on the surface and at the first sign of trouble your life will fall apart as you are swept away with the world's worries and concerns. Apply the effort to dig deep and do the work and you will have that peace that surpasses all understanding here, and when in heaven, the Father will say "well done good and faithful servant". Where's your foundation?

Robbie's comments:

We are deceived if we think being a Christian doesn't take work and effort on our part. Here the Bible is talking about having a deep foundation. There is no way we can have that deep foundation without work. Works are not what save us, please hear that clearly. However, if we desire to live in fellowship with God it takes effort. We will get out of it what we put into it. If we don't read our Bibles, attend church, pray often, hang out with other believers and participate in a good Bible study, we will flounder around in mediocrity and have very little, if any, effect in showing others Christ in our lives. I can look back in my life and know exactly how my walk was by how I handled certain situations in my life. I believe God brings circumstances in our lives to remind us that He desires that relationship with us. He is a jealous God and when we are not giving Him the time and attention He desires, He will make sure that we do. Unfortunately, that is usually in the way of a negative circumstance that turns us back to Him. Life is so much better when we keep our lives in balance. When I finally got this concept, and I mean really got it, my life started looking a whole lot different. When we build our houses, take the time to build a deep foundation. It takes longer and more effort but when the storm comes you will not be shaken.

Jim's comments:

I have put a lot of work into my foundation to be sure that I am standing on the solid work of Christ. I take my walk with the Lord seriously because He has done so much for me I can give Him nothing less than my life. Am I always perfect? No, but after I am knocked down by my flesh, the world, or Satan, I get back up and through Him; I am ready to fight another day because of my solid foundation.

Do You Allow A Little Leaven?

1 Corinthians 5:6 Your boasting is not good. Do you not know that a little leaven leavens the whole lump of dough?

In verses 1-5 we read that Paul has heard a report of sexual immorality in the church at Corinth. For some reason, instead of church discipline, they are proud of this immorality. Some commentaries say he may have been one of the church leaders. Paul condemns the act and how the church responded. Paul then administers the discipline which was usually carried out in front of the congregation. Turning him over to Satan meant casting him out of the church until he repented of his fleshly ways and then he could return.

Are there churches today that desire to be inclusive and not only wink at sin, but embrace it and boast of their openness? The situation here is not that we are to be sin free, but if there is open sin in the church with no sign of repentance, there is to be discipline. Open, un-repented sin, like a little leaven will spread throughout the church, bringing pain and suffering to the members and a slap at Christ and His suffering on the cross.

If we are to boast, it is about what God is doing in our lives. We boast in how He brought us out of bondage and into freedom. We boast in salvation and in our personal relationship in Christ. If we are strong enough to remove the leaven, then we can boast in Him, giving us the courage to do what's right. Do you allow a little leaven?

Robbie's comments:

There is a song called *Slow Fade* which, I think, is exactly what happens in our lives. Not just the church, but we see it in our government, our schools and sadly enough, in our homes. We didn't just wake up one day and notice that morals and values seem to be a thing of the past. It happened over time and continues to happen as we sit idly by and do nothing. It's time for us to get up and speak up. Those opposing Christian beliefs don't seem to have a problem with speaking up. Let's quit being passive and start being passionate.

Jim's comments:

I do my best to keep my eyes open to anything that will cause harm to my brothers and sisters in Christ. Sometimes it is hard to confront and I either ignore it or just pray about it. There is nothing wrong with praying over the situation but when He speaks and tells me to confront, I sometimes shrink back from doing what I know is right. That is a problem for me and a problem in a lot of churches. We do nothing when we know we should confront. If we would confront at the first sign of open sin, it would keep a lot of serious heartaches from happening.

Got Your Shine On?

Matthew 5:16 Let your light shine before men in such a way that they may see your good works, and glorify your Father who is in heaven.

Is your light shining brightly or beginning to dim? Do others see good works that glorify the Father or just another hypocrite? Do you act one way in church and another outside its doors? Or worse yet, is the real you the one outside the church doors?

Jesus is telling us that we should act in such a way that people will see a difference, a good difference. Our lives should be a shining example of what Christ has done for us and what He can do for others. Be attentive to the prompting of the Holy Spirit for opportunities to do good. Let Christ's love flow through you to affect those around you. The world is watching and they are keeping a score card. Who are you scoring points for? God? Yourself? Satan?

We must always remember that our good works are not for salvation, but because of it. We can do nothing on our own but through Christ... anything. We should be the first to offer a hand, a shoulder to cry on, or just the presence of being there when someone is hurting. We must not let the glare of the false light of the world make our light any less bright. Stay d.u.I. and let Him work through you. Got your shine on?

Robbie's comments:

Several years ago, Jim and I decided that we would go away, just the two of us, for an annual "marriage retreat". We go just for the weekend and take an inventory of where we are in our marriage, our walk with the Lord, our children, etc. We then set new goals about prayer, money, tasks we want to accomplish, etc. Sometime during the weekend God will give us a verse that touches us and sends a message to us. This verse, Matthew 5:16 was the verse for our first weekend. We have clung to it ever since. I do want my light to shine before men so they see my good works and glorify my Father in heaven. God's Word doesn't mean anything if we are not applying it to our lives. I would encourage you to find a verse for yourself or you and your spouse and start to live by it.

Jim's comments:

This verse is one of the verses I have turned into a prayer. What we need to understand is the world is watching us and we need to be different. We should let our light shine so others would see Christ and then the Father would be glorified. I try to do all things to the best of my ability so people will notice and then God can get the glory.

How Do You Smell?

2 Corinthians 2:14-15 But thanks be to God, who always leads us in triumph in Christ, and manifests through us the sweet aroma of the knowledge of Him in every place. For we are a fragrance of Christ to God among those who are being saved and among those who are perishing.

How do you smell? Are you the sweet aroma that fills the room with godliness, or are you the bland odor of mediocrity, or worse yet, are you that foul stench of discontentment? Take a good whiff of yourself.

Paul is telling the Corinthians to be thankful to God for their victories through Christ. We need to tell people of our victories in Christ and release that sweet aroma. It's that fragrance of Christ that is released when we genuinely share how we were, what happened (grace), and how we are now. As we continue to share what God is doing in our lives we will share the knowledge of Him in every place we go. How we spread that knowledge determines our smell.

The bland odor of mediocrity is released by Christians who go silently through the day minding their own business. They may have a bumper sticker or some other symbol to show who they are. They rarely speak up about moral issues because they do not want to offend anybody. They hardly ever share their faith and usually have few victories to share. They give God that one hour on Sundays and every once in a while send some money His way.

The foul stench Christians are quick to thump you with their Bibles. They will tell you what you are doing wrong but seldom offer a solution. They are condemning and quick to judge. They rarely share the Gospel because they are too busy telling you that you are going to hell. They think they are better than most, especially other believers. Their lives reflect very little joy. Which one are you? How do you smell?

Robbie's comments:

The key for me in this verse is the "sweet aroma of the knowledge of Him". The living Bible says that "He uses us to spread the knowledge of Christ everywhere like a sweet perfume". Of course we must first have knowledge of Him before we can spread the knowledge of Him. That is why it is so important to be in a good Bible study. I am very weak when it comes to knowing the Bible. I mean really knowing it. Knowing the history and cultures, not just concepts and generalities, is where I fall short. I am amazed at Jim's knowledge of the Bible. He is one of the most knowledgeable people I know. Not just the Bible, but knowledgeable about so much. I can learn something today and it's gone by tomorrow. I have always struggled with retaining things I have learned. I have to be taught over and over again and sometimes still don't remember it. I have to take it slow and steady and absorb it. If it takes a week to learn one verse, so what? That's one verse I know now that I didn't know before. If it takes me studying the same chapter or book over and over to get the concept and understand all about it then so what? At the end of however long it takes I will then know all about it. I want to be a sweet aroma and I know you do also.

Jim's comments:

I try to bring a sweet fragrance everywhere I go but it isn't always easy. Every day I try a little more to be like Christ. He was stern with the Pharisees and kind and gentle with sinners. One of my character defects was that I, quite frankly didn't like people. I don't tolerate stupid and thought most people were just that. God changed all that when I went through Tres Dias and now I truly love my brothers and sisters in Christ and I am learning to love the lost. I want to be that sweet smell that encourages the brethren and brings hope to the lost.

Are You Tempted?

James 1:14 But each one is tempted when he is carried away and enticed by his own lust.

Are you tempted? Are you drawn towards that which keeps you defeated? Are you carried away by a thought life that is less than pleasing to God? James states that it is of ourselves and not God who is doing the tempting (vs.13). We are tempted when we don't take every thought captive and allow them to linger in our mind. The longer they stay there, the easier it is to act on them. The temptation is of the flesh and can only be countered by the Spirit.

The best way to keep from being tempted is to keep our thoughts off of ourselves and on Christ. This is why prayer, Bible study, fellowship and serving are so important. If we make good practice of these, less tempting thoughts are apt to enter our minds. When they do, we will instinctively know how to handle them. The best defense against temptation is to stay on offense. Keep moving towards the goal of sanctification. Keep your eyes on what is good, and holy and righteous. Stay d.u.I.

We must always remember that the evil one will try and make us stumble. His main tool is to whisper to us about that which appeals to the flesh. He knows what buttons to push. Again, the four keys of prayer, Bible study, fellowship and serving keep Satan in check.

God will not tempt us. He may test us, but His tests will never be more than we can handle. If we fail the test, He will gladly let us take it again and again. Tests are to polish us and reveal our character. If we firmly place our trust in Christ and are obedient to the Holy Spirit, we can pass any test and resist any temptation. Are you tempted?

Robbie's comments:

I am tempted every day, how about you? I am tempted by food, overspending, television, letting my mouth react before my brain can stop it, just to mention a few. When I learned the concept of taking ever thought captive it made a huge impact on my life. I would try and immediately dismiss any temptation that did not need to be entertained more than a millisecond. I would sometimes say out loud "get out of my head!" Even though we have no control over the thoughts that enter our minds, we do have control over what we do with those thoughts. I still entertain way too many thoughts for way too long but I'm learning day by day. It's a process. It takes practice. It takes God. I can't do it alone. God is faithful to keep retesting us until we get it right! It's a good thing He doesn't give up on us or He would have given up on me a long time ago!

Jim's comments:

Do I get tempted? Yes, but that is not really the problem. The problem arises when I don't immediately take that thought captive. Satan, the flesh, and the world will always bombard me and try to get me off task. Staying d.u.I. keeps me moving forward and keeps my eye on the prize. I have to constantly think, who am I trying to please? Is it God, myself, or others?

Does God Know Your Wants?

Philippians 4:6 (Amplified) Do not fret or have any anxiety about anything, but in every circumstance and in everything, by prayer and petition [definite requests], with thanksgiving, continue to make your wants known to God.

Does God know your wants? I am not talking about your needs, those are already taken care of (Matthew 6:32). What do you want? What are the desires of your heart? What brings you happiness? What brings you pleasure? We need to make these known to God.

If we are not coming to God with our wants we have one of two options. Option one is to deny we have wants. We might tell ourselves that it is wrong to desire this or that. We may also deceive ourselves by thinking our wants are planted in our hearts by Satan. Option two is to go about achieving our wants on our own. We can struggle with debt or manipulate circumstances to get what we want. Let's deal with both of these errors.

The first issue of denying we have wants or feeling guilty for having them is a tool used by Satan to keep us down and uninspired. This verse clearly states we should continually make our wants known to God. He made us and He gave us our desires. The flesh may misuse these desires but if you bring them before the Father He will either grant them or remove them. Either way your wants our being met.

The second falsehood is acquiring them on your own. This pushes God out of the way as your supplier. Once this is done it is easy to slip into the world's ways of getting what we want. Debt, manipulation, not giving or tithing, stealing, or a host of other sinful behaviors will then be your means to your wants. We saw what happened in the Garden when they decided to get things on their own. Reliance on God for everything is what He desires.

Bring all your wants and desires to Him. Your desire for things, friends, money, love, and whatever else is on your list. There is not a part of your life you should not share with Him. If you don't share them with Him, do you really think He doesn't know what is going on in your heart anyway? Bring them to the throne and either get your desires or have Him remove them. Does God know your wants?

Robbie's comments:

I'm really good at this one! God knows all my wants. I pray for them often. Right now, I want this ministry to challenge other believers to walk daily under God's Influence. It's the only way to truly have the abundant life. I want to have enough money to give to others as God leads me. I want a new car as mine sits up at the local Post Office because when I came out of it yesterday it wouldn't start and Jim is pretty sure it needs a new fuel pump. Oh, and I want the money to pay for a new fuel pump! The point is that since God knows our hearts, He knows our wants anyway. We might as well start praying for them and about them. If we doubt whether or not our wants are lined up with God's desire to give them to us, prayer is a great place to start. Sometimes, I will think I want something but when I actually start praying about it and/or for it, God changes my heart. Be honest with God. His Word says that He will give us the desires of our heart, but it also says to seek Him first. When we seek Him first our desires will line up with His desires for us and blessings will abound. Seek Him first in all you do today.

Jim's comments:

Does God know my wants? Yes, and if He should ever forget I remind Him each day. I learned early on to take everything to the Lord in prayer. He either grants me my request or removes the want. I guess after being a drug addict and alcoholic for so long and trying to get everything on my own I learned I don't know what's best for me, but He does. I really do try to take everything to Him in prayer.

What Are You Leaving The Next Generation?

Judges 2:10 All that generation also were gathered to their
fathers; and there arose another generation after them who
did not know the LORD, nor yet the work which He had
done for Israel.

In verse 2 we read how the Israelites were disobedient to God's
instruction to conquer all the land He had given them. Those
Canaanites the Israelites did not drive out as they were instructed
they subdued and made slaves, but that's not what God told them
to do. The reason God wanted them driven from the land is they
worshipped idols and they would draw Israel from worshipping the
one true God. That is exactly what happened. After the generation
that entered the Promise Land repented and sacrificed to the Lord,
(vs.5), they served the Lord until their death (vs.10). The next generation would receive the punishment for turning away from God.

How is your disobedience affecting the next generation? Are
you allowing other gods in your life? Are you allowing other gods
in your house? What are the Canaanites in your life? What have
you allowed to dwell among you thinking you have made a slave of
them?

One area of our life that would affect the next generation is our
attitude about church attendance. Do we complain about having to
go or how long the sermon is? Do we talk about others while we are
there? How do we treat others outside the church doors? Do we act
one way in church and another when we leave? How do we treat our
family? Do we give cheerfully? Our children, as well as others, are
watching. They can clearly see hypocrisy. If that's what they think
Christianity is we will surely see our numbers dwindle and the next
generation will pay for that ungodliness.

We all must take a good look at our lives. Are we the salt of
the earth? How is our joy? Do we act like we know Him? The next
generation is depending on us to show them who Christ is. We must
not fail them or they will pay. This quote off a DC Talk album says
it best.... "the greatest single cause of atheism in the world today, is
Christians, who acknowledge Jesus with their lips and walk out the

door and deny Him with their lifestyle. That is what an unbelieving world simply finds unbelievable". What are you leaving the next generation?

Robbie's comments:

We as parents must take seriously what we are leaving the next generation. We must teach them the importance of going to church, reading their Bible, and praying. When Casey, Corrie, and Jamie were younger we would pray every night before going to bed. We would all kneel around the bed and pray together. Then we got busy, on different schedules, one excuse after another and stopped doing it. I think we, as a generation, are busy-ing God right out of our lives. We see the moral decay and it's only getting worse. We have to make sure we love on our kids. There are so many kids out there just starved for love and attention. It breaks my heart to see parents embarrass or degrade their kids. There are so many generational curses out there that must be broken. God has given us the responsibility for growing up this next generation. Maybe today is the day you start praying with your children, or reading them a Bible story or decide you are going to start going to church again, not just this Sunday but every Sunday. We can make a difference with God's help and our willingness.

Jim's comments:

What am I leaving the next generation? Hopefully a ministry that will help Christians realize their potential in Christ and lead fulfilling lives that will in turn draw others to Christ. I want to make a difference in believers' lives so they can make a difference and the chain will go on until Christ comes back.

Do You Give To The Saints?

1 Corinthians 16:1 Now concerning the collection for the saints, as I directed the churches of Galatia, so do you also.

This is not about tithing. It is not about giving to United Way or any other secular charitable organization. This is about giving to other Christians and Christian organizations that either need it or you know will use it wisely. The church in Jerusalem needed it badly.

Paul took up a collection for that church everywhere he went. They were very poor. Its members were under serious persecution from their own people, the Jews. When most Jews accepted Christ, their own families would have nothing to do with them. Others would not conduct business with them and many of their businesses were burned. These new Jewish Christians lost family, friends, homes and businesses all because they believed in the Messiah their own Scriptures promised. There was a desperate need for funds to support the church.

The money Paul was collecting was over and above what the Christians were giving to support their own local church. This type of giving is called an offering. The giving of alms is for the poor (Leviticus 19:9, 10). The second type of offering is the offering of First Fruits (Exodus 23:19) which today would be giving a share of any increase. Then there is the tithe which is ten percent (10%). Then there is the offering or seed giving. This is the least done today but the most rewarded. The more seeds you sow you more you will reap (2 Corinthians 9:6). An added benefit of giving is that it is the cure for greed. Greed holds on, giving shares.

After you tithe to your local church and give to those less fortunate, find a good Christian organization or ministry to give to. Plant seeds wherever and whenever you can. Not only will you be helping to spread the Gospel and the cause of Christ, you will also be creating a harvest for yourself later on. Do you give to the saints?

Robbie's comments:

I love giving. I love blessing people. I don't want the recognition or glory; I just want to bless others. We all hear about people who are in desperate need. I have a burning desire to help them. I wish I had lots of money so I could bless more people. I know many think having a lot of money or being wealthy is a bad thing. I say that is "rubbish"! What we do with money can be bad but it can also be very, very good. God wants to bless us and one of the ways He can bless us is with money so we can turn around and bless others. Does that mean we have to give it all away and not enjoy any of it ourselves? I don't think that message is anywhere in the Bible. If he made you a good carpenter, does that mean you can only build things for others and not build anything for yourself? If he made you a good cook, does that mean you can only cook for others to enjoy? I don't think so. We, too, can enjoy the blessings and gifts God has given us. Share them? Yes. Enjoy them? Yes.

Jim's comments:

Do I give to the saints? I try to give as much as possible. I have learned it's not always about money. Sometimes it is just to listen or give a smile and a kind word. I may even be asked to do something I dread, like help someone move. I never ask anyone to help me move therefore I won't have to return the favor. When it does come to money I give as much as I can and always try to listen to the Holy Spirit. As soon as I realized it all comes from Him it made it much easier to give.

Are You Courageous?

Joshua 1:7 Only be strong and very courageous; be careful to do according to all the law which Moses My servant commanded you; do not turn from it to the right or to the left, so that you may have success wherever you go.

Are you bold and daring? Are you brave and fearless? We should be. We serve an awesome God. Looking back to creation and then all the miracles through Exodus and then standing at the door to the promise land you would think it would be easy to be courageous. But is it?

Here we see God's recipe for courage. First, there is a warning - be careful, watch what you are doing. Be sure to do all that Moses commanded, which was the law, the Word, the Bible. Whatever name we use, our first lesson in how to be strong and courageous is to know God's Word. The next lesson is to live it. Do not turn from it either to the left or to the right. This phrase "turn to the left or to the right" means to be distracted and turn to our own ways. It can be from the flesh or from Satan. Knowing the Word is only part of the plan. You have to exercise it daily.

Now the result, that you may have success wherever you go. Success is the achievement of aims sought. Whatever you set out to do be strong and courageous by knowing the Word, speaking it boldly and letting it guide your steps. Keep it in front of you and you will not be distracted and stray from God's path. Are you courageous?

Robbie's comments:

I can tell you that the more I am in the Word, live the Word, and speak the Word, the more courageous I feel. When I am not in the Word I become a different person, not so bold or courageous. With God close by I feel as if all things are possible. Oh! That's because they are! Matthew 19:26 verifies it. We must be courageous and bold in our prayers. I have never prayed so boldly and courageously than when Jim was in the pit of his addiction. I knew God heard my prayers. I knew He would answer my prayers. I just had to keep believing even when I wanted to stop believing. Be strong, be courageous.

Jim's comments:

Am I courageous? At times I can be. If I am pushed into a situation it is easier because it gives me little time to think. Once I start to think I sometimes focus on all the things that can go wrong and then do nothing. Staying focused on God and His word makes being courageous a whole lot easier. I love having days where I don't have to think. When I am in tune with God and His plan and everything just seems to flow with very little effort. That is what happens when you are d.u.I.

Conclusion

How are your toes? We are not trying to step on anybody's; we are just bringing truth to help in your daily walk. It is so important to not let religious people put anyone or anything between you and Jesus. He is the One who did all the work and then He sat down at the right hand of the Father. The work of forgiveness is finished and now we can build on that foundation. It takes work to build a life that is pleasing to God but we don't do it alone. We have the Holy Spirit to help us shine and keep us from smelling too awful. He also helps us when we are tempted and when we need to confront.

How did you do on prayer? Do you take all your wants to Him in prayer so that you have something left to give to the saints? Are you leaving the next generation something besides all your stuff? Do you have the courage to leave them a godly legacy? Now is the time to start. Our God is the One who can change lives and work miracles. Let's continue on and ask God to speak to you and change you as you answer the next ten.

Chapter Four

Is God Speaking To You?

Are You Reconciled?

Colossians 1:21-22 And although you were formerly alienated and hostile in mind, engaged in evil deeds, yet He has
now reconciled you in His fleshly body through death, in
order to present you before Him holy and blameless and
beyond reproach.

A lot of people dislike verse 21 because they are "good people".
Maybe you don't lie, cheat, or steal. You don't cuss, cheat on
your spouse, beat your children, or a host of things "others" do.
You think you are fairly honest and you help people. Romans 3:12
clearly states there are none good, no not one. So, if we are not good
enough on our own, then we need to be reconciled.

The Amplified Bible uses "estranged" for "alienated" and
estranged means to divert from its original use, purpose or possessor.
That is exactly what happened at the fall. We were diverted from our
original use and purpose, to be in fellowship with God. Because of
that break we were diverted from our original Possessor.

So, although you do good deeds, what God really desires is that
you have a relationship with Him. Anything less than that is hostile
and evil in God's sight. As Isaiah 64:6 states, our righteousness is
as filthy rags.

Now we need a way back to God; a way to be brought back into harmony with our Creator. That way is Christ. I love how Paul says "fleshly body" so as to remind us that Jesus came to earth in human form as a man and died a horrible death and was resurrected for the sole purpose of cleansing us of our sins to be presentable to the Father. As believers, we are presented holy and blameless and beyond reproach. Are you in that right relationship with the Father, through Christ as Lord and Savior? I hope you are and you are now living a life beyond reproach. Are you reconciled?

Robbie's comments:

I am reconciled but only through the blood of Christ. There is no other way to be reconciled. There is only one way to God the Father and that is through the reconciliation of Jesus. Even though He died on the cross for everyone, we must accept that free gift He offers and enter into that relationship with Him in order to get to heaven. The Word is very clear that good works are not what gets you to heaven, although good works *should* be one of the results of your salvation. You can "good works" yourself to death and many people do think that is sufficient. The problem is they are wrong. The ONLY way to the Father is through the Son (John 14:6 Jesus said to him, "I am the way, and the truth, and the life; no one comes to the Father but through Me.") If you have not yet been reconciled back to God the Father, please do it now. It doesn't take a special formula, ceremony or prayer, just a willing heart. If that is your desire (praise God!) tell someone who can help you get started in your Christian walk.

Jim's comments:

I need to go back to these verses often because the everyday grind of life, the flesh, and Satan wear me down and I forget what God sees when He looks at me. He sees me as holy, blameless, and beyond reproach. When I choose to live in light of this truth instead of the lie, I can be used by God and my life is much more peaceful.

Had Enough Baby Food?

1 Corinthians 3:1-2 And I, brethren, could not speak to you as to spiritual men, but as to men of flesh, as to infants in Christ. I gave you milk to drink, not solid food; for you were not yet able to receive it. Indeed, even now you are not yet able.

Paul is writing to the church at Corinth telling them why he couldn't speak to them about the deeper Christian doctrines. They were still infants in Christ which has little to do with how long you have been a Christian. Maturity in Christ has everything to do with how much you live in the Spirit and how little in the flesh. Paul clearly tells them he cannot speak to them as spiritual men, but men of flesh. We have insight into how they were acting.

How often do you fall back into the flesh? What percentage of your day is lived in the Spirit? If it's only on Sunday mornings, the rest of your week will either be miserable or very unproductive for the Kingdom. We all need that solid food daily. That food that comes from reading the Word, prayer, solid Bible teaching, attending and serving in a local church, and fellowship with other believers. Of all of these, I believe prayer is most important.

If you desire to get off of the milk and onto solid food, start by being in the Word. Pray before you read that the Holy Spirit will reveal the truth and how to apply it to your life. Be around other believers. Pray with them and for them. Find a good Bible teacher then check his word with the Word. Most of all, pray about everything. Prayer opens the door to allow the Holy Spirit to do great works in us to keep the flesh in check. Remember, when we get to heaven, we don't get a new spiritual side, the flesh is just removed. We have it all now; we just need to access it. Had enough baby food?

Robbie's comments:

I think one of my biggest frustrations is seeing Christians still on baby food. I have to remember that there was a time in my life when all I was feeding on was baby food also. If I only knew then what I know now. We can live our whole lives on spiritual baby food. Believe me, I see many giving it a try. The problem is they are not being effective for the Kingdom of God and they are missing so many of the blessings that God wants to give them. Are they still going to heaven as believers? Of course, but God has so many wonderful plans for our lives here on earth. We have to be close to Him and walk with Him everyday. Let's get serious and eat some real food today.

Jim's comments:

I think it is quite obvious how I feel about these verses. This is the whole reason for the book and d.u.I. ministries, to get Christians to live in the Spirit and not the flesh. It does take some discipline at first but gets easier over time and actually becomes quite a joy.

Who Are You Imitating?

Hebrews 6:11-12 And we desire that each one of you show the same diligence so as to realize the full assurance of hope until the end, so that you will not be sluggish, but imitators of those who through faith and patience inherit the promises.

Who do you look up to? Who do you strive to be like? I know it is so easy to say "Jesus". He is our example but here the writer obviously thinks we need to find a human who is faithful and patient and living the abundant life. It is encouraging to see another Christian overcome, rise above and walk his talk. We can relate and apply this to our life on a human level. If they can do it, then we can too.

So again, who do you look up to? A sports hero? Movie star? TV personality or other media figure? How do they stack up against Jesus? Does their life reveal their faith and patience? We need someone we can look to who is the real thing so that we may have hope and not be spiritually lazy. Be careful not to pick someone that is at your spiritual maturity level or even slightly below. You will be inclined to feel content with your walk and not pursue the higher challenge.

We are to be careful and painstaking in our walk so we can realize the hope that Christ has for us, the full life He purchased, that faith-filled life that stretches us and helps others. Maybe someday someone will want to imitate you. Who are you imitating?

Robbie's comments:

There are a few people that come to mind immediately when I think of people who have helped me so much in my Christian walk and still do today. They have a maturity I strive for, Bible knowledge I can only dream of, and the true abundant life that I am starting to experience. We have to keep our dreams alive. Jim and I lead a community group for our church and we asked everyone one night "what God size dream are you waiting for God to do in your life?" There was not one person who had a big dream, or at least wanted to share it. I believe my God for big things. I am not ashamed that I have big dreams that only God can fulfill. When they come to pass, then I know that God and only God will get the glory and praise. I have learned so many things from others that are walking the talk. They are doers of the Word and not just hearers. God wants us to live the abundant life. I want to live the abundant life and I know you do too. We need to all keep striving for excellence in everything we do.

Jim's comments:

Who am I imitating? This one I struggle with because of my character defect of perfectionism. Part of me thinks there is no one out there doing it perfectly so why imitate them and another part of me thinks if I put in enough effort I can do it perfectly. You can see how this is a great defect and at times can be paralyzing, but I do stop and realize none of us are perfect so I try to glean the best from those I admire and remember we are all human and therefore prone to make mistakes. The main thing is to not put those you admire and are imitating on a pedestal.

Can You Pass The Test?

Psalm 26:1-2 Vindicate me, O LORD, for I have walked in my integrity, and I have trusted in the LORD without wavering. Examine me, O LORD, and try me; Test my mind and my heart.

These are two very bold verses. Can you honestly say to God, "examine me, and test my mind and my heart"? Would you be free from blame? Have you walked in uprightness of conduct? Could you be convicted of being d.u.I.?

David is asking God to vindicate him which means to defend successfully. That's not quite like going to trial with the O.J. jury. You can't pull the wool over God's eyes. He knows it all and still David says "test me". The reason for his boldness is he has trusted in the Lord without hesitation. Because of that steady dedicated trust, David walks in integrity which means wholeness and honesty. He is crying out "look at me and my ways and You will find me blameless".

Now, can you do that? Can you cry out to the Lord and say "test me"? Would you like to be examined by Him in this way? If we put our trust in Christ and allow the Holy Spirit to work in our lives, we can pass the test. If we stay in the Word, pray throughout the day, fellowship with other believers, and put our entire trust in Christ, we will pass the test. Can you pass the test?

Robbie's comments:

It is so amazing when you know that you are smack dab in the middle of God's will. You know, that you know, that you know, that you are passing the test. You are "connected". You are walking daily with Him. You are at peace. Everything might not be going your way or according to your plan, but you are still at peace. However, if you are like me, those times in my life have not been as often as I would like. I get easily distracted and I have always struggled with discipline. I can say without hesitation, however, that there is no better place than being "connected" to God the Father, but it takes discipline. Some days I pass the test and some days I don't. Thank God He gives us as many make up tests as it takes.

Jim's comments:

These verses are not about being perfect but about trusting God. I am learning to do this better each day. When I made the commitment to listen to God and quit my job I had to trust in Him. We cut our income almost in half so we are relying on Him for the rest. It does get scary at times but I have to remember who is trying to scare me; Satan. I believe I do well in trusting Him.

Are You Wasting Your Breath?

Matthew 10:14 (Amplified) And whoever will not receive and accept and welcome you or listen to your message, as you leave that house or town, shake the dust [of it] from your feet.

Have you ever felt like your words were falling on deaf ears? When I researched the phrase "shake the dust off your feet" I found it was meant to convey a warning of judgment. Jesus is using this opportunity to teach His disciples not to waste time preaching to those who will not hear. Their judgment is not in your inability to reach them, but their unwillingness to believe.

I have seen many Christians browbeat friends, co-workers, or relatives with the Gospel to no avail. Then they feel it was their fault that the others did not believe. We have to remember Who is doing the saving. Jesus said "no one can come to me unless the Father who sent me draws him..." (John 6:44). Our job is to preach the Gospel and most importantly, live it. Once the seed of the Word is planted, the Holy Spirit goes to work and it is the individual's responsibility to accept or deny the truth. We may run the risk of alienating those we are trying to reach with an overbearing message or a walk that does not match our talk.

The message here is to spread the truth through word and deed. We must not waste precious time by continued bombardment on a select few we desire to be saved, when there are many who are ripe for the harvest. Are you wasting your breath?

Robbie's comments:

God says that His Word will not return to Him empty (Isaiah 55:11). If we share the gospel with others, God will use it. We can't get caught up and distracted by the results, that's God's job. We can and should continue to pray for them and their salvation. It's tough when you have family members that are not saved and you continue to share your faith with them and see no results. Just remember, to share with them in love and not frustration. They are lost and don't understand, blind and do not see. We have to treat them like a blind person. Be patient, love them and never stop praying.

Jim's comments:

I do try to live this out, but part of the problem is another character defect from my past of not really caring for people. I usually just say "well I put it out there; it's up to them now". I actually do care about people now but have to remember my role is to speak truth and let the Holy Spirit do the work. One thing is for sure, unbelievers are watching what we do more than what we say. My good friend, Lorne Hulan, says "Spread the Gospel and use words if necessary".

Are You Timid?

2 Timothy 1:7 For God has not given us a spirit of timidity, but of power and love and discipline.

Are you fearful? Are you lacking in courage? Do you often find yourself saying "I wish I would have done this or said that"? Have you ever walked away from a conversation with someone and said "I had the perfect opportunity to share my faith but didn't"? This must be why Paul was writing this verse to Timothy. In verse 8 Paul says, "Do not be ashamed of the testimony of our Lord or of me". If we try to operate on our own strength we have every reason to be timid.

To be bold and share what God has done and is doing in our life takes power. That power comes from the Holy Spirit. He is our source of strength and ability to exercise our faith valiantly. Also, we need to share in love. Love for others will give us that power to communicate our beliefs effectively. We get that love from the Father through Jesus and expressed by the Holy Spirit changing our heart. We also get it from discipline. A disciplined walk is where we stay in the Word, fellowship with other believers, pray often and allow the Holy Spirit to work in us and through us.

If we have a spirit of timidity, it is not from God. Check the discipline of your walk. Are you lazy in any one area? God has given us the spirit of love, power, and discipline. We have to access that power by being d.u.I. Are you timid?

Robbie's comments:

I am timid in so many areas of my life. I am still not comfortable sharing the Gospel with a complete stranger like some can do. I've learned that's OK. I use to feel guilty about that but I've learned that not all of us are called to be evangelists. Should we be ready to share it at all times? Absolutely, but should I feel guilty that I didn't share it with the lady in front of me in the grocery store? Only if I felt God prompting me to tell her and I disobeyed. Not all of us are wired that way. If we are all out sharing the gospel with strangers there would be nobody to help those new believers grow. Now, if God tells me to share the gospel with a stranger, then I have to trust that He will give me the words to say and the confidence to say them and then I should be obedient.

I use to be very timid or perhaps too prideful, to share my story about being the spouse of an addict and alcoholic but God has changed that about me. I learned we all have a story to tell and there is someone out there that needs to hear it. Are you willing to share your story?

Jim's comments:

I do sometimes shrink back from confronting. Then there are times I can be totally overbearing and in your face. Both are wrong. I need to listen to the Holy Spirit and speak when He tells me and only what He tells me to say. Tim Goodman, another good friend of mine, is unashamed to speak his mind almost to a fault. I wish I could be more like him.

Do You Pray Scripture?

Romans 15:4 For whatever was written in earlier times was written for our instruction, so that through perseverance and the encouragement of the Scriptures we might have hope.

There is hope and encouragement in the Scriptures. There is hope in prayer. When you put the two together it's twice the hope and a whole lot more powerful. When you pray Scripture what you are doing is agreeing with God that His word is true and that you desire to live it out. It's great for beginners and old timers alike.

The concept here is to take a passage of Scripture and turn it into a prayer. I did this several years ago with Matthew 5:16. The verse reads "Let your light so shine before men that they may see your moral excellence and your praiseworthy, noble, and good deeds and recognize and honor and praise and glorify You Father, Who is in heaven". When I turned it into a prayer for my wife and me, it now reads "Father, I pray Robbie's and my light would so shine … glorify You Father who is in heaven". I later added Galatians 5:16 to the end of it. I pray this daily. After about six months of praying it, Robbie and I were doing things guided by the Spirit that were getting us a lot of praise which we of course turned back to the Father. Our lights were shining through what seemed like no effort on our part. The Holy Spirit gives us an idea, we run with it and the Father gets the glory.

My suggestion is to get two or three life verses and turn them into prayers. Then as the circumstances arise in your life, take other Scripture and turn those into prayers to fit the situation. If you are going through financial difficulties use Luke 12:29-31, trouble with those who oppose you, Luke 6:27. A problem with anger, Ephesians 4:26-27. If you know someone who is a little hard hearted, pray Ephesians 4:31-32, which would read, Father, I pray _____ would let all bitterness and wrath and anger and clamor and slander be put away from him along with all malice. Let him be kind to others, tender hearted, forgiving others, just as You in Christ have forgiven us. The situations and combinations are endless. Do you pray Scripture?

Robbie's comments:

I had never heard of praying Scripture before a few years ago when a lady from my church and I did a Beth Moore study on praying God's Word. At that point in my walk, I had always struggled with prayer. I never doubted its importance in my walk; I just had a difficult time doing it. Then I started praying Scripture. It opened my eyes to a whole new way of praying. When I couldn't find the words to say I would find a Scripture and pray it. When I was dealing with Jim's addiction and found it hard to pray, sometimes I would just find a Scripture and cling to it. Prayer is communicating with God. We talk to Him and allow Him to talk to us through the Holy Spirit, through His Word and through other people. If you struggle with how to pray or what to pray, I would encourage you to start praying Scripture. Take the Scripture and turn it into a prayer back to God. Your prayer life will come alive!

Jim's comments:

Do I pray Scripture? Absolutely! I have four Scriptures I pray daily and when the situation arises I find Scriptures that fit the situation and pray them. This is foundational for my walk and I highly recommend it for everyone.

Do You Want Your Children To Imitate You?

1 Kings 15:11, 26 (11) Asa did what was right in the sight of the LORD, like David his father. (26) He did evil in the sight of the LORD, and walked in the way of his father and in his sin which he made Israel sin.

This is a story of two kings. One who was an heir to the throne and one who talked his way to the throne. Asa, the great great grandson of David, did right in the eyes of the Lord while Nadab did evil and walked in the ways of his father, Jeroboam. It was Jeroboam who convinced the ten tribes to split after Solomon's death. Solomon's son, Rehoboam, was arrogant and sophomoric. When the northern tribes asked if they would be treated better under Rehoboam then they were under Solomon, he dismissed the advice of the elders of Judah and said "if they thought his father Solomon was harsh, they had better be on their guard for him." That's all the ten tribes needed to hear and they seceded and became the northern kingdom of Israel. Rehoboam was left king over the remaining two tribes that were called Judah.

Nadab (vs. 26) was the son of Jeroboam. Jeroboam was an opportunist and took Rehoboam's miscue as a way to power. He wasn't appointed by God nor had a bloodline to the throne. Jeroboam set up two shrines at old sanctuaries and put a golden calf at each for the people to worship. These events led the people away from God and led to the exile and eventual destruction of the northern kingdom.

Asa (vs. 11), grandson of Rehoboam, and a bloodline to the throne of Judah, did right in the sight of the Lord. His grandfather, Rehoboam, and father, Abijan, also set up idols to be worshiped but Asa rid the land of much of its idolatry and even had the queen mother deposed because she erected an idol. He was striving to be like his great great grandfather David.

The lesson we take from this today is what kind of person are we presenting for our children to imitate? Are you like Nadab, the smooth talker who will say whatever it takes to get what you want and willing to worship false gods so as to go along with the crowd? Or are you going to be the one, like Asa, and rid your house of idols and worship the one true God? Are you going to pass on the blood-line of Jesus? Do you even want your children to imitate you? They will find a role model. Who will it be? Do you want your children to imitate you?

Robbie's comments:

It depends on the day. Some days are definitely better than others. I started a Bible study last week at church and one of the verses we studied this week was Deuteronomy 6:7-8 (You shall teach them diligently to your sons and shall talk of them when you sit in your house and when you walk by the way and when you lie down and when you rise up. You shall bind them as a sign on your hand and they shall be as frontals on your forehead.)

It has only been within the last few years that I have really felt the hunger for God's Word. I think it is because Jim has such a hunger for the Word and such a gift of knowledge. We just love talking about Scripture. He and my Sunday school teacher, Brian, have taught me so much. We have studied scriptures, debated their meaning and just poured over them. That is one of the reasons it is so important to be in a Bible study with others. You get to talk about it, ask about it, and challenge each other. That part of my walk I would love to have my children imitate. Other things - not so much, but I'm working on them!

Jim's comments:

I can finally say that I would like my children to imitate me. I just want them to imitate the good things I do of course. This is talking about setting examples through your everyday actions that they can SEE what you believe and not just hear it. My children have seen first hand how I used to be and what happened since I started living d.u.I. Children learn way more by what we do then what we say. They are the first ones to see when our actions don't line up with our words.

Do You Love Money?

1 Timothy 6:10 For the love of money is a root of all sorts of evil, and some by longing for it have wandered away from the faith and pierced themselves with many griefs.

Do you love money? I do! Without it I could not feed, shelter or clothe my family. I could not give to my church or other organizations that do so much good in our community. I could not give to mission work to spread the Gospel globally. The more I have, the more I can do and can give. So what is the real meaning of this verse?

Let's start with the basics. Money itself is neutral. It is neither good nor bad. I can use it for good by providing for my family and giving, or use it for evil by spending it on addictions, hording it, or paying to have someone murdered. The love of money is not evil. However, the love of money can be the beginning of all sorts of evil. If you love money more than God, by putting the acquiring of it before Him, that is wrong. If you fail to realize it all comes from Him, that is wrong. If you neglect your family and your spiritual life to get more, that is wrong. If you resort to cheating and lying to get more or keep more, that is wrong. If you put your trust in money and not Christ, that is wrong. Paul clearly states some have wandered from the faith and caused themselves serious harm by desiring it so earnestly. So, is your love of money causing you to drift spiritually or causing outright calamity?

Do you love money because you can provide for your family without struggling? Do you love to give wherever and whenever possible? Do you realize it is a gift from God? Do you love it so you don't waste it? Have you increased your giving above ten percent? If your love for it hasn't caused all sorts of evil or much grief, I believe you understand the importance of money and how God expects you to be a good steward of it.

I have heard people say they are not greedy; they just want enough to get by on and pay their bills. They may not be greedy, but they sure are selfish. If you only want enough for your needs, how can you give to help others? If you say you don't love money, how does the amount you have or don't have affect your happiness? Everybody is happy on payday. The truth is, put God first, and then realize money's importance in the Kingdom. Get the most you can in a balanced, Biblical way. Then always let the Spirit lead in how you spend it, give it, and save it. Do you love money?

Robbie's comments:

I do love money. I love having it and I love blessing others with it. I wish I had a lot more of it. Some of us are under the impression that having a lot of money would be bad and for some that might be the case. Maybe God knows that we would not use it wisely or maybe God sees that we have not been good stewards of what He has given us so He sure isn't going to give us any more. Jim & I have put ourselves on a very strict budget. We have bills and outstanding debt that needs to be paid and since he is no longer drawing a steady paycheck we have to really watch what we spend. I truly believe God wants us to use what He has given us wisely. That is a Biblical truth. However, I don't think that means to be stingy with what God has given us or to not enjoy what God has given us. If we are debt free, tithing and giving as God instructs us to then we should not feel guilty in enjoying what God has blessed us with. I know many who judge others and how they spend their money. They criticize their brothers and sisters for living in a nice house, driving a nice car, owning a boat or a plane. Who are they to judge? Do they know how much time and money they give to their church, missions, other ministries and those in need? I think some, if not all, of the judgment here is jealousy. Money is no different than attitudes. They can both be used for good or evil. How's your attitude?

Jim's comments:

Do I love money? There was a time when I loved it more than anything else. Money is what bought me drugs and alcohol. It is what made me important in other's eyes and my own. It defined me and it was how I defined others. Now I know the truth about it and its importance in people's lives and in His Kingdom. I just need to keep Him number one and all these things will be added to me.

Can You Help?

1 Thessalonians 5:14-15 We urge you, brethren, admonish the unruly, encourage the fainthearted, help the weak, be patient with everyone. See that no one repays another with evil for evil, but always seek after that which is good for one another and for all people.

Can you help? Most people can and do help those less fortunate than themselves. But, could you speak to another believer of equal or higher social status whose behavior was wayward and could cause harm to the body of Christ or a member? Could you turn the other cheek if a brother offended you? Here Paul is telling us how to help our brothers and sisters so as to have an effective witness of the power of the Gospel.

We are to gently warn and admonish those who profess Christ but get off track. We are to encourage those new in the Faith who stumble in their walk. We help the weak and are patient with EVERYONE. If someone does us harm we must pray for them and if it continues we confront, but never retaliate. When dealing with believers we must always do what is best for the body, not ourselves or other individuals. This requires that we be strong in the faith or d.u.I.

So as you observe other believers, be ready to help no matter what the situation or how uncomfortable you may feel, because the good of the body is at stake as well as our witness. Can you help?

Robbie's comments:

I have such a hard time confronting other believers who are straying or getting off track. Most of us could use, at the minimum, a little encouragement to get back on track concerning some aspect of our walk. I know I sure could. I always feel like I have to have the perfect walk before I have any right to point out the flaws in someone else's walk, and that's never going to happen. First of all, we need to have earned the right to approach that person with our concerns and that comes with loving others and spending time with them. If some stranger walked up to you and told you something you needed to change in your life, you wouldn't give them the time of day. It's all about the relationship. When we genuinely love our brothers and sisters we can correct out of love. It still may not be easy. What it also does is help us examine our own walk. I probably don't have much credibility if my life is a mess and I'm trying to help you correct something in your life. Hopefully, there is someone loving me enough to help me too. Again, it's not easy for me either, but it gets less difficult with practice. I'll just keep practicing.

Jim's comments:

Another one I struggle with. I am good at encouraging but not so good at confronting. I will pray for others when they struggle but sometimes something needs to be said. God is working on me as I try to do it in love and not "in your face and what the heck is wrong with you" mode.

Conclusion

This time I hope we stepped on some toes. We really need to stress you are not good enough to get to heaven on your own. You never have been and you never will be. You need to be reconciled. After that comes discipleship so you can get off the baby food. Find someone who you can imitate so you will be able to pass the test and not be timid. Quit wasting your breath on the few you want to be saved and let your walk be an open invitation of the Gospel to all those who you come in contact with.

Again, we go to the prayer life. Would you like your children to imitate your prayer life? Do you work scripture into your prayers? Do you pray over all your money decisions? Here is where we really need to be different than the world. There is a fine line between loving money too much and enjoying what God has blessed us with. Keeping that line from becoming blurred is what allows us to be able to be good stewards and help others. As we continue on you may want to look for patterns in your answers that might point out some character defects that are hidden just beneath the surface. Be honest and allow the Holy Spirit to work. Next we'll get justified.

Chapter Five

Let's Get Justified!

Are You Justified?

Romans 5:1 Therefore, having been justified by faith, we have peace with God through our Lord Jesus Christ.

If you have a good dictionary, or an old enough one, you will find this phrase "justification by faith". It's listed under the word "justify" between "justification" and "justificative". It is defined as "gracious or merciful act of God by which a sinner who has faith in God's mercy is freed from the penalty of his sins and restored to God's favor". That is what we get from salvation; mercy, grace, faith, freedom, restoration and God's favor. Pretty awesome, isn't it?

As we read the verse above we also see the "how"- Jesus Christ. We first have to know we are sinners and separated from God before we can realize we need to be justified. Once that is established, we go to the "how". Faith in Christ. The end of the previous chapter talks about Abraham's faith and how it was credited to him as righteousness. Do you have that same faith in Christ? Do you have that faith that brings justification and peace with God? Are you justified?

Robbie's comments:

Sometimes I wonder if I really know what it means to be "freed from the penalty of my sins and restored to God's favor". I know that I am and I know how totally awesome that is. We know that the penalty of sin is death and that God's gift to us is eternal life with Him for those who believe in and put their trust in Jesus. I think it is the "restored to God's favor" that really blows my mind. He loves us so much. I'm not sure it is humanly possible to understand or grasp the depth of God's love for us. We can only compare it to the earthly love we have for others, whether that be our children, our spouse, or someone else. I know the depth of love I have for my children. When they hurt or get mistreated, it tears me all to pieces. The love God has for us does not even compare to the deepest love we have ever known. The sacrifice Christ made on the cross made it possible for us to be restored to God's favor. God sacrificed His Son! I can't even stand it when someone hurts one of my children's feelings. Wow! What love He has for us! My mind cannot even comprehend.

Jim's comments:

I feel totally at peace with God. I do not believe that He is angry with me or that He is just waiting for me to screw up so He can whack me. I fully believe that Christ has justified me and through my faith in Him, God and I are okay. I am a friend of God, He calls me Fred! (That's for my daughter Jamie).

Do You Have A Good Defense?

1 Peter 3:15 But sanctify Christ as Lord in your hearts always being ready to make a defense to everyone who asks you to give an account for the hope that is in you, yet with gentleness and reverence.

If you were put on trial for impersonating a Christian could your defense attorney provide enough evidence to prove that you really are a Christian and not just pretending? Do your actions account for the hope that is in you? Are you acting so differently that people will ask you for an account of the hope that is in you? This is the best way for the Gospel to be spread.

Let's take a look at our workplace. How do we interact with our co-workers? Let's go to the verses leading up to 3:15 to see how we should act at work. We are to be harmonious and kind hearted (vs.8). We don't return insult for insult and we bless those who do insult us (vs.9). We keep our tongue from evil and deceit (vs.10). We seek peace when turmoil is at hand (vs.11). We do not fear those who try to intimidate us (vs.14). Think about your workplace. Do your unbelieving co-workers act this way? Do you?

Most workplaces are rumor and gossip mills. Insults fly about the room and there is backbiting and deceit to get ahead. We, as Christians, are to be so different others cannot help but to notice and ask why. Then we are to be ready for the defense of our actions. This is the perfect opportunity to explain how we used to be and what changed us, or Who changed us. We are to be gentle and not overbearing in presenting how the Gospel has changed us. We also show a reverence for Christ and the work He has done in us. This approach is far better than Bible thumping and acting as if you are better than them. I don't believe you should have to tell people you are a Christian. They should already have seen it.

Is your Christianity so personal no one else sees it? Do you try not to offend anyone with it? Or, are you the rock solid one who is so different everyone wants to know why? Do you have a good defense?

Robbie's comments:

I try to be encouraging, kind hearted and harmonious at work. I try to get along with everyone and not be confrontational. But to be honest, nobody has ever asked me what makes me different or why don't I react to certain situations like everyone else. Maybe I don't look as differently as I think I do. If anyone were to ask me, would I be able to tell them? I am not one of those that think my Christianity is a personal thing between me and God. On the contrary, I think it needs to be shared in a loving and kind manner, but the truth of the matter is, I very rarely share my faith with unbelievers. It makes me wonder if I have really prepared myself to give a good defense? A new employee and I struck up a conversation the other day. I had gotten some hints from some things she had said that she might be a believer. After talking for a few minutes I discovered she was a believer, but she sure didn't believe the same things I did. She was all about the "warm fuzzies" and told me not to get too caught up on "God". "God" could be anything we wanted it to be. God is found in where we draw our strength. Everyone has their own definition of God. She also said we could always trust our heart. It would never let us down. Every red flag in my body was going up. I was able to tell her that my truth came from the Bible. That was my basis for truth. My right and wrong came from God's Word. Her right and wrong just came from whatever made her feel good and brought her inner peace. I could tell the Holy Spirit was guiding my tongue and it was such an awesome feeling. It made me realize just how important it is to be ready to give a good defense.

Jim's comments:

My being a former alcoholic and addict, and the change He made in me is a pretty good defense. I still have to have Biblical knowledge to back up my claims and be ready to share them when the situation arises. Once I share the hope that is in me comes the real test. Can I live out my faith so people will know it's real?

Who Are You Working For?

Ephesians 6:5-7 Slaves, be obedient to those who are your masters according to the flesh, with fear and trembling, in the sincerity of your heart, as to Christ; not by way of eye-service, as men-pleasers, but as slaves of Christ, doing the will of God from the heart. With good will render service, as to the Lord, and not to men.

Slaves of Biblical times can be somewhat compared to employees of today for several reasons. Some were paid, and most were treated fairly. They could acquire legal rights, own other slaves, and had the power to conduct their own business. Some sold themselves into slavery because of debt. How many of us are working at a job we dislike and feel a calling to go elsewhere but can't because of our debt? Maybe we cannot afford to take a cut in pay to do what God desires because of our debt for "stuff". In a sense, we are enslaved to debt.

Regardless of why we are at our jobs, or who we work for, we are to work as slaves to Christ. We need to do our job professionally, courteously, efficiently, and to the best of our ability. Paul says not by way of eye-service, meaning just when we are being watched. There is no qualifier about how our employer is supposed to act. As Christians, we are to be different. If we try to do as little as possible or just enough to get by, we are no different than the world.

We must always remember who we are working for, Christ, not man. If we do our best, He will reward us. Hard work, fiscal discipline and much prayer will get us out of slavery to debt. Then we will be in a position to do what God desires us to do. And the old saying is true "if you do what you love, the money will follow". Who are you working for?

Robbie's comments:

I am one of those who are working for "debt". I love my job but do not feel like it is God's calling for my life. My God size prayer for many years now has been that I could be a stay at home mom. I knew it would take a miracle because there was no way financially that could happen without a miracle from God. Well, my youngest daughter, Jamie, is graduating from high school in less than three months and for whatever reason He has not answered that prayer. He has brought Jim home through the ministry and for that I am very thankful. I still wait for the day when I can join him fulltime in the ministry. That will take a big financial blessing which we are still hoping and praying for. In the meantime, I will continue to be thankful for the job I have and do it to the best of my ability knowing I am still there for a reason and a purpose.

Jim's comments:

I have always tried to conduct myself at any job I had by giving my best at all times, (that is when I wasn't stoned and drunk). I got my work ethic from my Dad, a very hard worker. My daughters Casey and Corrie have that same work ethic also. That is why even before I was a Christian I gave my all, but now it is much more so. He is who I work for and no matter what we do for a living it is God who provides the paycheck. When we put it in that perspective it should be easier to give our all.

Do You Know God's Plan For You?

Jeremiah 29:11-13 "For I know the plans that I have for you," declares the LORD, "plans for welfare and not for calamity to give you a future and a hope". Then you will call upon Me and come and pray to Me, and I will listen to you. You will seek Me and find Me when you search for Me with all your heart.

Do you know God's plan for you? Here we see His plan for the nation of Judah in the midst of their defeat and exile to the Babylonians. Jeremiah 29:4 tells how it was God who caused them to be carried away. Any reading of the Old Testament prophets will reveal why He caused their captivity - disobedience. The prophets preached time and time again turn from your idols back to the one true God. So even though He caused it, He still had plans for a great future.

So what is God's plan for us as believers? Plans for peace and not evil, plans for future and a hope. His plans are that we will call upon Him and pray to Him. The plan is that we would seek and find Him. This is all He has ever wanted from us - a relationship. Out of this relationship comes our peace, our future, and our hope.

If your life is not peaceful and you feel you have no future, it's examination time. Look closely at your relationship with Him. Have you turned to idols? Is there anything in your life you've put between you and God? It may even be something good like your children, your spouse, your church, or serving others. We saw what it did to Israel and Judah as the people of these nations slowly turned from Him. If you turn from Him, he will do something to get your attention. Remember; listen when God whispers because you don't want Him to raise His voice.

Do you call upon Him for your daily needs and wants? Do you pray to Him? Do you search for Him with all your heart? If we do as verse 14 says, He will be found by us. So, if your life is falling apart and everything is upside down, remember His plans for you... plans for peace and for a future. Do you know God's plan for you?

Robbie's comments:

Why God allows some things to happen we will never know on this side of heaven. I do not believe that everything that happens is God's plan or His will. I do not think it was God's will for my brother, Scott, to take his own life at the age of 33. However, I do believe God allowed that to happen as a result of Scott's choices over the years as a drug addict. However, I do believe that God can take any bad situation and have good come from it. That is where our faith comes in. We have to know that He is God and we are not and His plans and His ways are not our ways. We also have to realize that God is not Santa Claus. We have to do our part and then God will do His. The verse says we must call upon Him, come to Him, pray to Him, seek Him and search for Him with all of our heart. I would encourage you as you read your Bible to understand your role in your relationship with God, the Father. There are two sides to any good, successful, meaningful relationship. It took me many years to realize that I have a part to play in my relationship with God. He so desires us to be close to Him. Seek Him today.

Jim's comments:

My goal for those who read this book is that you will find God's plan for your life. He created you for something and when you find it that is when the real joy begins. I won't say it will be easy, but it will be fulfilling.

Are You Convinced?

Romans 8:38-39 For I am convinced that neither death, nor life, nor angels, nor principalities, nor things present, nor things to come, nor powers, nor height, nor depth, nor any other created thing, will be able to separate us from the love of God, which is in Christ Jesus our Lord.

What a joy it is to be loved like that. I only wish I could love like that. These verses are a description of unconditional love. You too can be loved like this.

Most of what we fear in life is listed in this text. If and when they do come to pass, He still loves us. When we die, we are in heaven with Him. In life, He loved us while we were still sinners. Angels cannot separate that love. Neither can demons. What we do today or tomorrow can't separate us. Even when governments try with all their might, they can't. No matter what we accomplish or how bad we fail, it can't. Also, no other person can separate us from God's love if we are in Christ Jesus.

Are you persuaded and satisfied by proof of this love? Do you feel it and know it? As believers we need to be convinced so as not to be tossed to and fro with everything that happens in our life. Paul tells us God's love is unconditional and unending. I pray you feel that love. Are you convinced?

Robbie's comments:

He said it. I believe it. I am convinced...enough said.

Jim's comments:

I am convinced of God's unconditional love for me. I know there is nothing I can do to keep Him from loving me. I do wish I could love like that, to love people regardless of their attitude, lifestyle, demeanor, or anything else. I am getting better though.

Do You Rejoice With Others?

Luke 15:5-6 When he has found it, he lays it on his shoulders, rejoicing. And when he comes home, he calls together his friends and his neighbors, saying to them, "Rejoice with me, for I have found my sheep which was lost!"

I am going to take these verses a little out of context to make a point. This is a parable about the joy in heaven over one sinner repenting (vs.7). A parable is an earthly story with a heavenly meaning. For the parable to make sense to the one listening, the earthly story had to have some truth to it. Apparently when something good happened back then they rejoiced with others. Today, not so much.

We tend to live a lot of our life in isolation, not wanting to share any of ourselves with others. We definitely do not want others to know of our shortcomings or character defects. If we can keep them hidden we can keep our happy, smiling Christian masks on. The problem is if we don't share our struggles how can we share our victories over them? In other words, if we are not willing to tell people that our sheep is lost, how can we rejoice with them when it is found?

The reason we need to share our struggles and the victory over them is to show others that victory is possible. We need to rejoice with others when God does anything in our life, big or small. Just think of the people who can gain hope by you sharing your victory. Revealing our struggles not only releases the power they have over us but actually makes victory possible. Keeping it in the dark gives the power to Satan, exposing it to the Light releases that power and then God gets the glory.

The next time you struggle, tell somebody. Revealing our secret sins is risky, so be sure the one you tell is someone you can trust, someone who will help you and encourage you, but will not excuse or rationalize your behavior. Then when God does anything in your life, tell people and rejoice with them. Share the hope that is in Christ. Do you rejoice with others?

Robbie's comments:

I was just thinking about this today. The last Sunday of every month my church has a "Praise and Worship" service where we come together, sing praise songs and share the praises of what God is doing or something He has done in our lives. I usually don't share because I am very emotional and usually cannot get through one sentence before starting to cry. But what I realized is "so what if I'm emotional?" Shame on me for not sharing what God is doing in my life. I lived so much of my life in isolation and thinking that people don't care and don't want to hear the struggles in my life that I also believed they didn't want to hear the victories either. I have now learned that others need to hear both. Just like it says above, we need to share both our struggles and our victories. I love rejoicing with others. I love to hear and see what God has done and is doing in the lives of others. Why do I think they wouldn't want to hear what God is doing in my life also? I will start sharing at "Praise and Worship" every month!

Jim's comments:

It is easy to rejoice with others over our new car, TV or some other thing. Do I share my struggles with others so that I can share the victory with them as well? Most times I do. That is part of how God removed my addiction and alcoholism. It was through sharing my struggle with my brothers and sisters in Christ at one of our Praise and Worship services that God started to work in removing it from me. Now that He finally has, we have been rejoicing together ever since!

Are You A Prayer Warrior?

Ephesians 6:18 With all prayer and petition pray at all times in the Spirit, and with this in view, be on the alert with all perseverance and petition for all the saints.

How is your prayer life? Are you a prayer warrior or do you just throw up "fox hole" prayers? Do you pray at all times or only when in need? It is obvious from this verse how we are supposed to pray. So how do we get there?

Christianity is a personal relationship with the Creator of everything. Communication is essential for any relationship. That is what prayer is. To pray means to ask earnestly, petition God, request, appeal, implore, beseech and worship. Seeing how communication is two way, after praying comes listening. How will we know His answers if we don't listen? We need to live a life of prayer.

Above, Paul states we are to pray on the alert and with perseverance. We don't just toss up meaningless words or words to sound important. We pray what is in our heart. We pray for others. We pray for our enemies. Prayer or praying is mentioned over 520 times in the Bible. This does not include "petition" or "supplication". Just look at how Jesus relied on prayer. It is the most under-utilized tool in most Christians' lives.

We are also to pray in the Spirit. This means to keep our flesh out of the way. This will come as your prayer life matures. After praying enough fleshly prayers, the Holy Spirit will show you how self absorbed your prayers are. Not that you shouldn't pray for yourself, but be careful of asking with wrong motives (James 4:3).

Paul also tells us to pray at all times. How is that possible? One way is to make quick little prayers a common response to anything life throws at you throughout the day. Also, if you live d.u.I. you can make your life a prayer. Prayers can never be overestimated in the believer's life. Are you a prayer warrior?

Robbie's comments:

I can tell you without hesitation that this was the weakest area of my Christian walk until just recently. Like most Christians, I was heavy into prayer when my life was in turmoil and I had no other options. Why is prayer usually our last resort instead of our first? Prayer is how we communicate with God, so when I wasn't praying, I wasn't communicating. I have since learned that not only is prayer important, it is essential. Jim and I, as a last resort I might add, started a prayer group at our church. We were so frustrated with our church for many reasons but did not feel God telling us to leave the church so we decided to commit ourselves to prayer. We invited a few other couples to join us on Sunday mornings before church to pray over our worship team, our pastor and in each room of our church (5 classrooms and the nursery). I went in with expectations of seeing change in the church. What I discovered was that God made a change in me immediately. From the very first Sunday I started seeing people and situations in a whole new light. Keep praying... God wants to hear from you.

Jim's comments:

I am a prayer warrior. I know how prayer has changed my life and those around me and I realize its importance in the life of the believer. I think it is one of the most neglected tools in the church. That is part of my passion for this book and d.u.I. ministries.

Are Your Teens Glad We Are Not Under Law?

Deuteronomy 21:18-21 If any man has a stubborn and rebellious son who will not obey his father or his mother, and when they chastise him, he will not even listen to them, then his father and mother shall seize him, and bring him out to the elders of his city at the gateway of his hometown. They shall say to the elders of his city, this son of ours is stubborn and rebellious, he will not obey us, he is a glutton and a drunkard. Then all the men of his city shall stone him to death; so you shall remove the evil from your midst, and all Israel will hear of it and fear.

This may seem a little drastic but I would be willing to bet they didn't have teen gangs back then. What these verses really show is the importance of raising godly children. In those days there was very little tolerance for rebellious youths. As a society they knew defiant teens, if left unchanged, would turn into antagonistic adults. They were so worried about what these unruly teens would become and how that would affect the next generation they were willing to have their own children stoned to death!

As we look around today we see the results of undisciplined youth. Murders are committed by younger and younger children every year. Outright acts of defiance of authority and lack of respect for their elders are an epidemic among our youth. School behavior is out of control. My daughter, Corrie, is a teacher in a public school and some of the stuff she has to put up with would have gotten me expelled in the blink of an eye, and it did. There are few rules and most of them are not enforced. This is a topic for another book, possibly later.

This law was not in place to keep kids from having fun or because the elders were mean spirited. They knew if this next generation would not yield to the authority of the day, as these teens got older, this same disrespect would cause all of their community harm. I am not saying the law was good. The concept was right but the punishment a tad harsh.

What do the verses mean to us now? If you have children, work with children or just know some children we must realize the importance of discipline, especially self-discipline. The ability for our children to respect authority and trust it is paramount to our society. Look at what the sixties produced. It starts in the home and love is the most important part of discipline. If you love your children you will want what is best for them. A healthy respect for the consequences of wrong choices is a good start. Tell them and show them often how much you love them, set healthy boundaries, explain the consequences for going outside those boundaries, and then keep your word if they do. Then ask them, "aren't you glad teens are not under law.

Robbie's comments:

I have heard it said many times that growing up today is harder then when we grew up. That is said with every generation. I am sure it was said by my parents when I grew up and it will be said by my children when they become parents. I don't think the problem is the children. I think the problem is the parents. We are raising a generation of parents who think, for whatever reason, it is everyone else's responsibility to raise their children. From daycare, to school teachers, to the government, to the church, etc. These children then become parents and the problem gets worse with each generation. The things that go on in the schools today and what kids get away with astonishes me. We will have no choice but to suffer the consequences of what, we as a society, are allowing our children to get away with. Children need love, discipline, and boundaries. More and more are not getting any of the three which results in trying to find their identity in anything or anybody that will give them the attention they so desire. Raising good kids starts with being a good parent. It is our responsibility to raise our children. It is a huge responsibility and we will mess up at times, no doubt about it. But being grounded in our faith first is where we need to start. God will give us the wisdom on how to raise our children if we seek Him first.

Jim's comments:

We, as parents, have tried to raise our children as per the Bible. I think raising a child to be a balanced and well functioning adult is a responsibility every parent should take seriously. We would have a much better society if every one did so. If your children become believers so much the better but that is a decision they have to make on their own. We, of course, can strongly recommend it and through our actions can help in that decision to accept Christ.

Is Your Cup Running Over?

Luke 6:38 Give, and it will be given to you. They will pour into your lap a good measure—pressed down, shaken together, and running over. For by your standard of measure it will be measured to you in return.

Do you lack? Do you have just enough to get by? Do you struggle from week to week? Do you have a lot of friends? Is your cup half empty? Jesus is telling us how to have a full to overflowing life. The answer is easy - GIVE! One of the paradoxes of the Bible is you have to give to get. Then you give that to get more. If you want friends, give friendship. If you want love, give love. If you want money, give money. Giving is the antidote to greed. Greed is to hold on to, giving is to let go of.

Jesus also adds that how you measure out, you will receive. I believe this is more of a heart issue than an amount issue. If you give money just to get more for yourself then it won't work. If you give grudgingly or inconsistently, it won't work. If you try to impress others to win friends, it won't work. If you manipulate loved ones, it won't work. It has to be Holy Spirit inspired giving. Obedience to the Spirit will result in an overflowing cup. Obedience to the Word and prayer needs to be your standard of measure. Remember, give and it will be given to you. Is your cup running over?

Robbie's comments:

The only way I can have Holy Spirit inspired giving, whether it is money, friendship, time or love is to be living daily under the Influence of the Holy Spirit. For me that means discipline. That means forming habits that just become second nature. It is never discussed in my house whether or not we are going to church on Sunday morning. It's a habit. I use to struggle and forget to pray about things or I would use prayer as a last resort. It has now become a habit. It is now a constant in my life. How does that happen? It comes through repetition and discipline. Unfortunately, not all of my Christian walk is so disciplined. There are others areas that I am still working on. If your cup is not running over in a particular area of your Christian walk, whether it be giving, friendship, prayer, spending time in God's Word, or serving others, to name a few, just keep practicing. Do it even though you don't feel like it. Before you know it, it will become a habit you won't want to live without.

Jim's comments:

We try to give as much as possible, whenever possible. This includes our time as well as money. One thing I know for sure when times get tough and we pull back our giving it always gets worse until we make the commitment to give no matter what.

Ain't Scared?

Psalms 27:1 (Amplified) The Lord is my Light and my Salvation-whom shall I fear or dread? The Lord is the Refuge and Stronghold of my life-of whom shall I be afraid?

Are you afraid of anyone or anything? Is there something or someone keeping you up at night? Do you have a constant feeling of impending danger or evil? There is such a thing as healthy fear. Going to the dentist, a cab ride in New York City, or an I.R.S. audit are a few examples. But seriously, healthy fears keep us from making terrible mistakes. What David is talking about is a paralyzing fear that keeps us from being an effective Christian.

David writes that the Lord is his light. Light is used symbolically in the Bible to describe God's presence and favor. John 3:19 is a contrast between light and darkness and good and evil. What David is saying is that God is always with him, He is on his side, and He is keeping away evil. Is that how you feel? Is the Lord your protection and your fortress or is He who you run to once you make a mess of things on your own? If it is the first, then whom shall you fear?

When we put our trust in Jesus Christ we have that Light, that presence that is the Holy Spirit. We should fear no one or any circumstance. We have our faith in the One who will never let us down. He is our salvation. He is our refuge when the going gets tough. He is our stronghold in the midst of a sinful world. Faith not fear should rule the Christian's life. Ain't scared?

Robbie's comments:

I just got finished studying in my Bible study how God is our hedge of protection. He wants to be our refuge and strong tower. Why is it then that so many of us, including myself, run to Him last instead of first? When I have exhausted all other avenues, I then surrender it to God. God wants us to come to Him first, not last. I'm getting better because my prayer life is so much stronger than it used to be. When I would read about how we are to be in constant prayer to God (pray without ceasing), I thought that was just foolishness to think that someone could pray without ceasing. I would have to stay at home all day in order to pray all day. I think what it means is that we are to be in a prayer-like frame of mind all day. When something crosses our mind, we should immediately shoot it up to God in prayer. Our frame of mind should be thinking of God first. Now I am praying to God all day. Prayer is just having a conversation with God. Talk to Him throughout your day. Thank Him for the blessings He gives us each and every day. When someone comes to your mind, pray for them. When it's raining, thank Him. When someone makes you mad, pray right then for them and the situation. Don't make prayer something you just do when you wake up or when you go to bed. My prayer is that you will make prayer something you do all day long. It will become so second nature to you that you won't even realize it. We will fear less and trust more as we spend more time with God. God is bigger than the boogie man!

Jim's comments:

Another one of my character defects raises its ugly head. I do not like to tell people "no" or disappoint them in any way so my fear comes when they call and I either do not want to do it or know that I shouldn't because I can't. I sometimes struggle with this but I am getting better thanks to caller I.D. Seriously though, it is tough for me to say "no" because of another defect, I want people to like me. Again, through God's power I am getting better.

Conclusion

Are you starting to see some of the same questions asked from different angles? We do this because it is a very good interrogation tool. If you have ever been questioned by the police you will know what I am talking about. When asking the same question using different words the police look to see if you answer the same every time. Our goal is to do the same. We want you to be sure of your salvation, sure of your walk, and sure of what you believe and that it is truth. That is why the first question of each chapter deals with salvation. We want you to be sure.

So, are you justified? Can you give a good defense of that justification? Are you convinced of God's love and can rejoice with others over it? Do you know God's peace and do you rest in it so that you are not kept awake at night worrying? If you are a prayer warrior the answers to these and most other questions in life become a little easier.

The questions "Is your cup running over?" and "Who are you working for?" deal with stewardship issues. There are quite a few money questions in this book because the use of our money needs to set us apart from the world. Here we have to be different in how we earn it, save it, spend it, invest it, and give it. The question about teens is more of a social issue than anything else, but it could be used to keep your teens in line. Hopefully, the next ten will lead to some serious self examination.

Chapter Six

Need A Drink?

Are You Still Thirsty?

John 4:14 But whoever drinks of the water that I will give him shall never thirst; but the water that I will give him will become in him a well of water springing up to eternal life."

This passage plus the ones before and after it contain so much Biblical history, cultural realities, and truths about who Jesus is that it would take pages and pages to explain it all. But, I will try to bring at least one truth from it. Jesus is the water, and without Him, you will experience an unquenchable thirst.

Throughout the Bible water is used many, many times. Just the miracles of the Red Sea and the Jordan River, the water pouring forth from the rock for Moses, the priest using water for ceremonial cleansing as a symbolic spiritual purification are a few examples. Rain was a sign of God's blessing plus the fact that plants, animals, and humans need water to survive.

Symbolically, thirst describes spiritual longing (Psalm 42:1). It's that deep, deep down inside feeling of emptiness; that emptiness that we all try to fill with something... anything. It's that God-shaped hole that only He can fill. It's that thirst that wasn't there before the fall.

Are you still thirsty? Have you accepted Christ as your Lord and Savior? If you haven't I pray you would. Pray to accept Jesus. Believe that you are a sinner and Jesus died for your sins and that belief in Him brings us back into a right relationship with the Father. Read your Bible and find a good Bible believing church to serve in and be a disciple. As you grow and mature in Christ your thirst will be quenched. And when it's all over you will have that eternal life with Him in heaven. Are you still thirsty?

Robbie's comments:

I, too, pray that if you have not satisfied that thirst by accepting Christ as your Lord and Savior you will do that now and begin that relationship with Him that He so desires. If you have already accepted Him as your Lord and Savior I pray you will continue to satisfy that thirst by walking with Him daily. As human beings we must stay hydrated. What do we do when our body tells us it is thirsty? We drink something. Well, as Christians, we must stay hydrated as well. What do we do when our spirit is thirsty? We must hydrate it with God's Word. There is no thirst quencher like reading God's Word. Sometimes that means just picking it up and reading a verse or two and sometimes it means sitting down and really digging deep. If we don't drink from it on a regular basis we start getting dehydrated and lose our focus. Stay hydrated today.

Jim's comments:

I no longer have that thirst deep inside me that continued to ask why. Why am I here? What am I supposed to be doing? Is there a God? I have drunk the Spiritual water and I have quenched the thirst.

Do You Have A Plan?

Luke 14:28-30 For which one of you, when he wants to build a tower, does not first sit down and calculate the cost to see if he has enough to complete it? Otherwise, when he has laid a foundation and is not able to finish, all who observe it begin to ridicule him, saying, "This man began to build and was not able to finish".

In this teaching Jesus was explaining to the crowds the cost of discipleship (vs.26-27). This illustration can also be applied to our lives. Do you have a plan, or do you just wing it? Are you someone who starts lots of projects but rarely finishes any?

If you want to build a life that is pleasing to God, you need a plan. Goals, immediate, short, and long term are the foundation for an effective plan. You must first realize the goals need to be from God, about God, and include God. This will come as a result of much prayer, Bible study, godly counsel, and a little experimentation. Patience will also play a key role.

I have met many people who excitedly tell me God has told them to do a certain task. When I see them a short time later, they have dropped that project and are on to something else. God does not work that way. He does not want to see His children ridiculed. They are either not hearing God or are too impatient to wait and listen for the rest of the plan.

Once God reveals a task we need to pray for what we can do immediately. Keep a journal and when reading your Bible, praying, or talking with others, write down any ideas that pertain to your plan. Any choices you make should always answer this question "Will this lead me closer to my goals or farther away?" Set aside prayer time just for the project and keep track of answered prayers and where He remains silent. Keep in mind any talents or abilities He has gifted you with that will make the plan flow. Act when prompted by the Holy Spirit. Do not be afraid to set big goals as long as they are from Him.

Once you have a plan, stay on it. Always remember God's time-table is not the same as ours. Continue to stay focused on the task at hand and read His Word, pray, fellowship with other believers, and serve in your local church. Be obedient and you will be amazed at how smoothly the plan will come together. Do you have a plan?

Robbie's comments:

When Jim and I started the prayer ministry at our church over a year ago, Cindy, one of our prayer partners gave Jim and me a prayer journal. She encouraged us to keep track of our prayer requests and how God answers them. When we started the ministry, my pastor's wife, Judy, told us to be sure and keep a journal of our journey so we could look back and see God's plan develop all along the way. There is nothing like having a plan that you know is from God, and then start pursuing that plan and watch God show up. We had to count the cost when Jim quit his job to pursue the ministry fulltime. We have bathed this ministry and this book in prayer from day one. The first thing Jim and I did when we started the ministry is to get a group of our closest and dearest friends and asked them if they would join us in doing nothing but praying about the ministry. Jim sends out a weekly email to our prayer partners with an update on the ministry, the book, and prayer requests. We have a plan. It's God's plan and it has been so exciting to see God work and make it happen and to be able to share that with our dearest friends that have come along side us and encouraged us every step of the way. We absolutely could not have done it without their support and encouragement. God is good!

Jim's comments:

I do have a plan. I have goals, short, medium, and long. I have a vision of what He wants me to do and how to do it. The key for me to stay on track is that constant connectedness from being d.u.I. God does not change and when He tells me to do something I must do it. He may leave some details up to me and that is where goals come in. Goals can keep me on track to make sure I don't stray from the objective. I do have a plan but it really is His plan.

How Do You Rate Yourself?

Romans 12:3 For through the grace given to me I say to everyone among you not to think more highly of himself than he ought to think; but to think so as to have sound judgment, as God has allotted to each a measure of faith.

I often hear people misinterpret this verse. They say you shouldn't think too highly of yourself. That's not what Paul said. He said don't think more highly of yourself than you should. The Greek means "not to have an exaggerated opinion of your own importance". The real heart of this verse is to take an inventory. List the good and bad and see how you rate. Don't compare yourself with others. If you want someone to compare yourself with, try Jesus.

The key to seeing if you are yielding yourself to the Holy Spirit is an inventory. Take stock of your character defects and look at ways to start eliminating them. Next, list your strong points and continue to grow in these as well. Do you earnestly desire to spend time with God and in His Word? How do you treat people? How is your joy? Are you laying up treasures in heaven or on earth?

A spiritual inventory is crucial to your walk. This should be done at least once or twice a year. After your inventory, pray to have God remove your defects and continue to build on your godly characteristics. Pray for growth, plan for growth, and pray for God to show you more ways that He can use you. Listen for the Holy Spirit because God wants you to be like Christ. How do you rate yourself?

Robbie's comments:

I have to say that I have never written out a moral inventory. I know I should and I know there are plenty of things that I need for God to remove from me. I don't think I am one to compare myself with others in a way that says I'm better or I'm worse. I admire many things about other people and strive to be more like that. I also see many things about people that I know I don't want to be like, and I know there are things about me that others don't want to be like either. The key for me is to strive to be better each day, keep building on my strengths using my gifts, and keep working on my character defects.

Jim's comments:

I continually rate myself. I keep a journal that I write in daily. As I periodically go back over it I can see growth or stumbling blocks. I even keep an exercise journal that has how much I weigh everyday and if I lifted weights or did an aerobic workout. I am constantly evaluating myself to be sure I am where God wants me to be.

Can You Restore Someone?

Galatians 6:1 Brethren, even if anyone is caught in any trespass, you who are spiritual, restore such a one in a spirit of gentleness; each one looking to yourself, so that you too will not be tempted.

When you see a brother committing a sin, do you a) look the other way, b) minimize it by saying nobody is perfect or c) chastise them and then toss them aside? Here we have instructions on just how to handle the situation.

The first instruction is you have to be spiritual. This actually means responsive to and controlled by the Holy Spirit or to pick a phrase I like "d.u.I.". Being controlled by the Holy Spirit you will not let the flesh reign and say or do something foolish. Plus, if you are not controlled by the Spirit, how can you have the credibility to confront? This does not mean you are perfect. It means just what it says "led by the Spirit". He will tell you what to say. He will show you what to do. You may not have time to go pray about it or consult others on what to do. This is why it is so important to be d.u.I. We never know when God will use us. If you are not daily under the Influence, this will allow Satan an opening. He will quickly point out something you did in the past and then say "how can you say anything to your brother?" The doubts will start to flow and nothing will be said to the offender which allows him to drift further from God.

So if you are guided by the Spirit and the situation arises, Paul urges that we use gentleness. We must first explain that what they are doing is wrong. They may not even know it. We must gently take them to God's Word to show why it is wrong and then guide them back on track, again using Scripture. All of this is to be done without an air of superiority. We have been in the same boat also.

We must also be attentive to the fact that we may be drawn in by them. Misery loves company. They may try to say that they are under grace and all is forgiven. Paul warns us to keep watch of our own walk so as not to be tempted also. If they can pull someone else into their sin, it brings a bit of legitimacy. We need to be strong and say "sin is sin".

We must always be alert and ready to help another believer when they fall. We must do it discretely, gently, and lovingly. We must treat them as we would like to be treated in the same situation. The only way we can help is if we stand strong and stay d.u.I. Can you restore someone?

Robbie's comments:

Gentleness has never been one of my strong points. I tend to either ignore or want to say "you idiot". I don't suggest either of those. It is difficult for me to confront my brothers and sisters when I see them openly and consistently doing something that I know to be wrong. I do believe that if I step out in faith, God will give me the words to say and the courage to say them. I guess my fear is I don't want them to think I am trying to be superior in any way. I don't want to come across as "I'm better than you" because none of us are better than the other. However, I do believe we need to keep each other accountable. That is not easy for me, but I have to keep working at it and know that God is there with me and will guide me.

Jim's comments:

I try to be a help to those I know who are struggling. Sometimes I don't need to say anything, just be there. My good friend, Tim Wood, and I once drove 180 miles one way to confront a friend of ours. We only talked for maybe ten minutes and then prayed with him, turned around and headed home. All we can do is make the effort and leave the results up to God. We can't fix anybody, but we can open the door for God to make a grand entrance through, just by showing someone we care.

Do You Do Good?

Galatians 6:9-10 Let us not lose heart in doing good, for in due time we will reap if we do not grow weary. So then, while we have opportunity, let us do good to all people, and especially to those who are of the household of the faith.

Do you do good? The Greek meaning for this word "good" is acting nobly and doing right. As you go throughout the day, do you do what is right or what is easy? Are your actions generous, honorable, and lofty? That is the definition of "noble". Can you do it day after day and not grow weary? Can you do it when it appears that you are not reaping any benefits from it?

Paul assures us we will reap if we do not lose heart and grow weary. We never know who is watching and what impact we will have on their day or their life by simple acts of doing what is right, something as simple as taking care of the "left wherever" shopping cart or letting someone out in front of us in traffic. We, as Christians, should be doing good always for other believers, but Paul also says to do good to all people.

Paul also states we should take every opportunity to do good. I know it is especially hard when nobody is watching, but God still is. If we are d.u.I. we will see many chances everyday to do good. We can most certainly start at home with those closest to us. I bet if you look, you could easily do ten good acts by noon in just one day. We must let the Holy Spirit speak to us and be attentive to His prompting. It will not only make your life more of a joy to live, it will affect those around you also. Do you do good?

Robbie's comments:

As I write this early in the morning, I am going to try today to do ten good things before noon. I would challenge you to do the same. Even if nobody is watching, God is. It makes me think about Debbie, a lady in our church who just recently moved. We have a problem in our church getting people to serve and show up for things such as this. To be honest, our church can be very apathetic at times. Imagine the surprise when about 40 people showed up to move her. It was one of the quickest and easiest moves I have ever seen. We had her old house loaded up, moved and unloaded into her new house in a few short hours. I could only imagine what her new neighbors were thinking as they saw us all congregate at her new house. What a testimony to God's love. Others were watching, I am sure of it. That's not why we did it but God certainly used it.

Update: I did about 3 "good" things before I got to work yesterday. Then I forgot all about it until I was driving home last night. I'm trying it again today.

Jim's comments:

I really do try hard to do this. From something as simple as holding doors open to letting others out in front of me in traffic. Just a smile sometimes does wonders for others. Sometimes I do get so caught up in my own life I do not even see others around me and that is when it is time to regroup and put things in perspective. I want others to say about me "what's wrong with that guy, no one is that nice?"

Are You Wasting Time?

Ephesians 5:16-17 Making the most of your time, because the days are evil. So then do not be foolish, but understand what the will of the Lord is.

How do you spend your time? Working? Sleeping? Playing? Eating? Hanging out? Watching TV? Etc. There are many activities where we can distribute our time. Do you have God time and then everything else? Do you spend a little time with Him in the morning and then leave Him in your quiet place until the next morning? How do we make the most of our time?

No matter what we are doing, God wants to be involved. Whether working or playing, eating or sleeping, talking or sitting quietly, He desires fellowship with us. If we are doing things that we don't want Him involved in, that is a whole other issue. When we are working, we are working as unto the Lord. When we eat, give thanks. When we play and laugh, thank Him for the happiness. When we watch TV, be careful of the content and how much we watch. He is with us whether we acknowledge Him or not.

Making the most of our time is to consider His ways in every-thing we do. The Greek actually means "buying up each oppor-tunity". See every activity as a means of fellowshipping with the Father. The world's ways are evil and we are to be in the world but not of it. Don't be foolish thinking we can please God with a little time each morning and then a little extra on Sundays. Include Him in all your activities and it will be easier to discern His will for you. Being a Christian is a 24/7 deal. Are you wasting time?

Robbie's comments:

I think we all waste time to some degree. That is one reason why it is very difficult for me to accept "busy" as an excuse for things. I know personally I waste time. I got up early this morning writing this (and I am not a morning person!) because I feel like I wasted too much time yesterday. Yesterday was Sunday and after church I chilled on the couch and watched TV most of the afternoon.

Not that watching TV is bad. We can't work 24/7. However, I could have balanced some writing with some TV. Again, it all goes back to choices. I chose to sit around and be lazy, and for me, that was wasting time. I am going to try and not waste time today.

Jim's comments:

I do try to keep God involved in everything I do. I try not to waste time and there are times when it is okay just to chill. One of my problems is the T.V. I can sit down to chill for a few minutes and, if I am not careful, two hours will go by. This is why a journal is so important to me. It lets me see what I have been doing with my days.

Do You Confess?

James 5:16 Therefore, confess your sins to one another, and pray for one another so that you may be healed. The effective prayer of a righteous man can accomplish much.

Do you confess? This verse is talking about confessing to one another, not to a priest. I don't have a problem with admitting your faults to a priest, but I do have a problem with asking one to forgive your sins. Christ has already died for our sins and they are forgiven by God. It is finished! What James is talking about is our sins against each other.

The word "confess" in both Greek and English is not about saying "I'm sorry". It is about agreeing that what was done was wrong. It is also about acknowledging faults. You can confess your sins to the one you hurt or you can simply confide in a brother a secret sin you harbor and wish to quit. The surest way to release a stronghold of sin in your life is to confess it. Just saying it out loud releases a lot of its power over you.

As we read in this verse, after confessing comes prayer. What a wonderful way to restore fellowship by admitting we wronged our brother and then praying with them. I believe it will not only heal relationships but harboring sin and ill will towards others leads to all sorts of sickness. James goes on to say how confession can lead to effective prayer that accomplishes much.

So much of what is wrong in the church today is because of unconfessed sin, either against God or each other. We need pure hearts and clean hands. We need to acknowledge our faults and wrongs to those we have hurt. We need to agree with God that our behavior and motives were wrong. Jesus has done all the work. We just need to accept it, live it, preach it, and teach it. It's called grace. Do you confess?

Robbie's comments:

Sometimes it is difficult for me to admit I am wrong. It's not that I don't know I am wrong. I just have a hard time saying it. I have a huge issue with pride. Admitting wrongdoing is not something that comes easy for me. I'm better than I was but nowhere near where I need to be. Sin definitely loses its power when it goes from darkness to light. This is another reason we need each other. I lived in isolation for many years and it is a very lonely place. That is why it is so important to have someone you can talk to... a friend, a pastor, or a mentor. Hopefully, they will not judge you, but love you and walk with you.

Jim's comments:

It's hard to confess when I am never wrong! I will give you all time to quit laughing, especially those of you who know me. Seriously, I do try to be the first to admit fault. Sometimes even if I don't think I am the one at fault. I don't like bad vibes so I try to keep from offending people and if there is the slightest chance I have, I try to be quick to apologize. Sometimes I can be sarcastic which can hurt others and I will not even realize it. Thankfully, I have Robbie, my wife, to point it out when I do.

Have You Cleaved?

Genesis 2:24 (Amplified) Therefore a man shall leave his father and his mother and shall become united and cleave to his wife, and they shall become one flesh.

Have you cleaved? To cleave means to adhere closely, stick fast, cling. I know this is easy to do when you first start dating. When you first fall in love you are inseparable. What happens? The Word says once you cleave you are to become one flesh.

The responsibility for marriage is on the man's shoulders. That is why he is to leave his father and mother. It is also his responsibility to keep the marriage together. He is the one to cleave to the wife. He is the one to adhere closely to her. He is to stick fast and cling to his bride. Also, the union is indissoluble because they are to be one flesh. Not a partnership, but one, a single unit. Even when man tries to separate this one flesh, through divorce, you never end up with the "wholes" you started with. Something is missing from both.

In Ephesians 5:33 Paul writes that men are to love their wives as they love themselves and the wife to respect her husband. That word for respect in the Greek means "to notice him, honor him, prefer him, venerate, esteem that she defers to him, praises him and loves and admires him exceedingly". Most husbands that I know value what their wives say. A friend may call me an idiot and it doesn't bother me. If my wife does, I am devastated. How can a husband love his wife as himself if he doesn't love himself because of the picture in his mind painted by a wife who doesn't "respect" him in the way Paul wrote about in verse 33? That is why the old saying is true "behind every good man is a good woman".

We men are also to love our wives as Christ loved the church (Ephesians 5:25). This means we are to die for her if necessary. There is no sacrifice too big for us to make for our wives. Also, Christ would never abandon His church. Christ would never cheat on His church. He would never abuse or make fun of the church. We are to love our wives as Christ loves the church whether they do their part or not. If our wives don't submit to us, we still need to submit to Christ just as He did to the Father.

As for the sexual side of marriage we read in Genesis 2:25, they were both naked and not ashamed. We should be pleasing to each other in our appearances; comfortable in our nakedness. When we were dating, we always tried to look our best, why change? Proverbs 5:19 is good advice "A woman should satisfy her man with her breasts and he should be exhilarated always with her love". Have you cleaved?

Robbie's comments:

Our church offers every other year a "Marriage Without Regrets" class taught by my pastor, Mike and his wife, Judy. Jim and I took this class several years ago when we were fairly new to the church. He was still drinking and lying about it and I was isolating myself and didn't have any true friends. We were struggling. On the outside, it didn't appear too bad but on the inside we were a mess. Judy told us ladies the first week that we were now one flesh. We all hear that in our wedding vows but all of a sudden the meaning became clear to me. We were one flesh. One single unit as noted above. I learned that God hates divorce and he can restore any marriage. He is God. When people ask me why I never divorced Jim, I tell them I did in my mind many times but Judy told me I couldn't so I didn't! I know sometimes we think our marriage is hopeless but God sees it differently. He can and wants to make your marriage strong and grounded in Him, but again it takes diligent work on our part. It takes constant prayer and surrendering to Him when we feel like nothing is happening and prayers aren't being answered. It's hanging on to Him when we have nothing left to hang on to. When we give up, I believe God is weeping and saying "but I had so many blessings for you on the other side if you had just stuck with me". God has united you as one. Stick with it. It will be worth it, I promise.

Jim's comments:

I have an awesome wife and an awesome marriage. It was not always this way. God was always there when I wasn't. He held my wife up. He kept her strong and faithful and she knew that He would fix me and make things right. And He did! We are one flesh. There is no one I would rather spend time with or who I trust more. She completes me.

Do You Put In More Than All These?

Mark 12:42-43 A poor widow came and put in two small copper coins, which amount to a cent. Calling His disciples to Him, He said to them, "Truly I say to you, this poor widow put in more than all the contributors to the treasury".

In verse 41 we see Jesus sitting down opposite the treasury observing the giving. What we need to realize is that today He is still observing the giving. He sees what we put in, but more importantly, He sees what we keep out. He knows of the toys we have. He knows the debt we have to buy things we don't need to impress people we don't like.

Whenever I talk with someone about giving, I am quick to point out that their giving is between them and God. Next, I will tell them that ten percent (10%) is just a good place to start. I know we are not under the Law to tithe even though the tithe was started before the Law. Genesis 14:20 states Abraham gave Melchizedek a tenth and that was about 600 years before Moses and the Law.

Your giving is a heart issue. If you are new to giving, give as much as you can and pray about what you should do in your finances to be able to give more. Those that have the means should give at least ten percent and then pray about giving more. Remember, it's not all about how much you give, but also what you do with what you have left over. Trust God with your finances. It all comes from Him anyway. For those who struggle with greed, the quickest way to conquer it is to give. Then you will find, once you start to give, you will start to get. Then you can give more. Do you put in more than all these?

Robbie's comments:

I love giving. However, I struggle with giving out of faith when I really don't have it to give. Jim is so much better at this than me. God is always faithful and always blesses the giver. I'm learning to let it go and see what God can do. He never lets me down. I hear all the time about people who sow that seed of faith, who give when they don't have it to give and God is always faithful and multiplies the gift. So why is it so hard sometimes to let go of it? It is a faith issue for me. Am I really trusting God? It's easy to give it when I have it. What about when I don't? What about the extras in life that I have that I really don't "need"? They are not a necessity of life but I of course, am not willing to give them up. You all know what I am talking about.... cell phones, cable TV, TV in general, computers, and the list goes on and on. I am really without excuse. What about you? If some of us would just start with giving something to our local church what a difference it would make. Start somewhere. God will bless your giving and your gift.

Jim's comments:

Again I could refer you back to the other times we talked about money in the book, it is all about putting money in the proper perspective. Prayer and a total reliance on Him is the sure way to keep money in its proper balance. I cannot be foolish and give all I have and not be able to support my family. I also cannot confuse supplying every "want" of my family with our needs.

Do You Have The Victory Of Da'Feet?

Proverbs 4:26-27(Amplified) Consider well the path of your feet, and let all your ways be established and ordered aright. Turn not aside to the right hand or to the left; remove your foot from evil.

Are you constantly getting off the path? Do you ever stop and seriously think about the path you are taking? Does it reflect the wide gate or narrow gate? Are your ways ordered by the Spirit or the flesh? Are you being pulled in two different directions at once? Do you have the victory of da'feet?

I believe there are two sides to this Proverb. One is the physical side. Are you letting your feet take you to places you should not go? The second is spiritual. Is your way of living lining up with God's Word?

On the physical side, are you going where you should not go? A recovering alcoholic does not need to go to a bar just to shoot a game of pool. It would be foolish to put himself in that situation. Do you, as a Christian, allow yourself to be near things that can tempt you and cause you to sin? I know the mind is what tells the feet where to go but the point is are you allowing your mind to tell your feet to take you someplace where you know nothing good can come from it? That is why this Proverb says "Consider well the paths of your feet". Stop, think it through and consider the consequences. Is it pleasing to God or not?

The second meaning is your spiritual path. Are you living in the Spirit or the flesh? Are you focused on God in everything you do? Do you allow Satan to pull you to the left or the right? Satan does not have to get us to do evil; all he needs to do is get us a little off track so that we are not as productive in the Kingdom as we could be. Consider all of the activities which you are involved. Some may even be at church. If they are not what God wants you to be doing then you are side-tracked. You may be serving in an area you wanted to but God did not want you to. He may have been drawing someone else instead, but you rushed in before they could. Listening to God is "having your way ordered right". Being where he wants you to be will keep you from having to remove your foot from evil.

To stay on the right path we need to be in His word, praying regularly, fellowshipping with other believers and partaking of the Lord's Supper. Doing these we will be more apt to hear His voice and stay on the path. Do you have the victory of da'feet?

Robbie's comments:

Where have my feet taken me lately? Have the steps I've taken been where God wanted me to go? Sometimes the answer to that might be obvious and sometimes it's not so clear. I know I have to get up and go to work every morning (until God blesses me with being able to stay at home) but those choices I make about where I go and what I do outside of my obligations are what I really have to think about. I love to shop but if I don't have the time and/or money to spend, then I should not be walking into a store. Sometimes, my flesh will have me rationalize in my head that it's OK and then I end up feeling guilty whether I buy anything or not. I still have wasted my time if not my money. I love to watch TV but should I be doing something else more productive with my time? I'm not saying it's not OK to unwind and relax watching a favorite TV show, but when I have to flip through every channel just to find something to watch; maybe I should find something more constructive to do. Ouch! That one hurt a bit. The point is we feel so much better when we are not wasting our time but using it productively for God's purpose and glory. I want to have the victory of da'feet!

Jim's comments:

I know first hand how just being where you shouldn't can cause all sorts of problems. They say in A.A. when you are in recovery to change your playmates and playgrounds. Part of my struggle was returning to the same old playground and then the same old thing would happen. I need to always be aware of where I am physically and what path I am on spiritually. That is why my journal is so important to me.

Conclusion

That chapter was serious inventory time. The questions deal with your plans and how you see yourself and if you think you are doing good and not wasting your time. Is there anything you need to confess to someone? These are all issues dealt with by a good inventory. If you don't know where you're going how will you know when you get there? How will you know if you are on the right path? A self inventory is at the heart of any good recovery program but it is also essential for all believers. God gave us a purpose and if you are still here you're not done yet. You need to know that purpose and be zealous about it. God is a God of excellence, not mediocrity, and self examination helps us eliminate bad inventory and build good inventory which glorifies Him. Let's jump into the next ten as we build that good inventory.

Chapter Seven

Out With The Bad And In With The Good!

Do You Know You're Forgiven?

Colossians 2:13 When you were dead in your transgressions and the uncircumcision of your flesh, He made you alive together with Him, having forgiven us all our transgressions.

Do you know you are truly and completely forgiven? This is a truth many Christians struggle with. They just don't think God can or will forgive them. They don't feel forgiven. This is a main tool that Satan uses to keep us from being effective for the Kingdom. I will demonstrate through Scripture the finality of our forgiveness.

Christ loves us and released us from our sins by His blood (Revelation 1:5). Throughout the Bible blood always had to be shed to cover sin. That's all animal blood could do – cover it. It took the sinless One to shed His blood to make one sacrifice for all time (Hebrews 10:12). He personally bore our sins in His body on the cross (1 Peter 2:24). He came for one reason – to take away our sins (1John 3:5). It is finished (John 19:30). We are forgiven. Now all we have to do is accept it and live in it.

Now that we know He did it, let us explore why He had to do it. Hebrews 10:3-4 reads "but in these sacrifices there is a reminder of sins year by year. For it is impossible for the blood of bulls and goats to take away sin". So God put in a plan for Christ to become the final sacrifice for the world's sin (1John 2:2). He became our propitiation. Propitiation is the removal of wrath by offering a gift. The wrath of God, at sin, is clearly taught in the Old Testament and continues in the New (Romans 1:18). The Father provided the gift for us (John 3:16). This was a once for all sacrificial gift to us. We cannot bring Him out and crucify Him again. It is done! It is over! We are forgiven! Now let's live like it!

If we continue to let Satan rob us of the freedom of being forgiven, we become useless for God's purpose. I have seen many Christians beat down by guilt because they don't understand the free gift of being forgiven. I see many Christians asking God for forgiveness. Why do we ask for something we already have? When the Bible says to confess our sins it means to agree with God about our sins. Agree with God that what we did was wrong and pray for the Holy Spirit to keep us from repeating it. Our sins were forgiven over 2000 years ago – past, present, and future sins. We need to quit asking for what we already have and start living in freedom. Do you know you're forgiven?

Robbie's comments:

We must know that we are forgiven if we are to have peace and be effective Christians. What do we have to offer others if we walk around feeling guilty or unworthy? Even if we don't feel forgiven, we are. Even if we don't feel God's love, it's real and it's true. Sometimes we need to put away our feelings and just accept God's Word. He says we are forgiven. Nothing will change that fact. If God says it, it is so, and He says we are forgiven. Now, let's start acting like we are forgiven. No more guilt. No more shame. Let's live in the freedom Christ came to give us.

Jim's comments:

I am 100% sure of my forgiveness. Many of you might not realize what a comfort this is to me. Because of my past I did some pretty horrible things. I did them to strangers and I did them to loved ones. I did them to everyone I came across. In the back of my mind I knew I was doing it to God also. His laws are the ones I was breaking. What a relief it is to know, without a doubt through the Cross, I am forgiven. I pray all who read this book get this point if they get anything at all "You Are Forgiven!"

Do You Obey Or Sacrifice?

1Samuel 15:22 Samuel said, Has the LORD as much delight in burnt offerings and sacrifices as in obeying the voice of the LORD? Behold, to obey is better than sacrifice, and to heed than the fat of rams.

This is the story of how King Saul thought he could do it his way instead of God's way. He had clear instructions from God, through Samuel the prophet, to go and kill all of the Amalekites and their animals (vs.3). Instead, he spared king Agag and the best of the animals (vs.9). Then when busted by Samuel he blames the people and says "we are going to sacrifice them to the Lord" (vs.21). The Lord wanted them sacrificed His way, on the battlefield, not Saul's way. Saul thought since he wasn't going to be obedient he would make up for it by sacrifices. This event led to him losing his kingship. To obey is better than sacrifice.

Let's fast forward 3000 years, the once for all sacrifice has already been made. All we have to do is be obedient. Most of us have a hard time with that. The flesh so desires to do it our own way that we either disobey God, or like Saul, half do it His way. We even have the Holy Spirit to help us accomplish God's instructions. We also have His Word and other believers to help us.

Do you get caught up in sacrificing instead of obeying? Do you promise to give more money? Do you promise to never miss church again? Are you trying to please God by sacrificing your time and money to appease the guilty feeling of disobedience? If you are a Christian, it is His money and His time anyway. He doesn't want or need your sacrificial gift. He wants your heart. If He has that, obedience is easy. Listen to His voice and stay grounded in His Word. Attend and serve in a good Bible preaching church. Fellowship with other believers, then when He gives you instructions, you will be able to carry them out. Obedience leads to a fuller, richer life here, and a greater reward in heaven. Do you obey or sacrifice?

Robbie's comments:

I have learned a lot about obedience over the last few years. I have learned the blessings that come with obedience and the pain and misery that comes with disobedience. The Bible is full of promises from God. We tend to only dwell on the promises or the end result without reading the complete verse or verses that explain how we get those promises. It is through seeking Him first. It is through living His Word (which we must first know it before we can live it). It is through calling on Him. It is through remaining faithful. It is through believing Him. It is through obedience.

Jim's comments:

I try to be obedient as much as possible but when I'm not, I go confess. I understand He wants me, not my disobedience and then a sacrifice. Confession is part of my Morning Prayer routine. I think back over the day before and if there is anything I shouldn't have said or done, I confess and ask Him for the power to overcome it and not do it again. I do not ask for forgiveness because that has already happened on the cross.

Who Ya Gonna Call?

Psalm 50:15 (Amplified) And call on Me in the day of trouble;
I will deliver you, and you shall honor and glorify Me.

This is a message to everyone, believers and non-believers alike. Anyone who calls upon the name of the Lord will be saved (Romans 10:13). That is what God desires of us. He desperately wants a relationship with us. That is why He sent His Son. The Holy Spirit is drawing us to call upon Him. When we call, He is faithful to reply.

As believers, we should be calling on Him for everything. No matter how small the details, if it is a concern to us, it is a concern to Him. He wants our day ordered around Him. He desires to be a part of everything we do. If we are not continually calling on Him, then we are calling upon the flesh. Anything that is not of faith is sin (Romans 14:23). If we continue calling on our flesh instead of Him the trouble will come, then He will get our attention and we will call out to Him. What I am talking about is self-induced trouble. Those we can avoid by being d.u.I.

As for non-believers, God is waiting for them to call also. After trying it your way, the world's way, your momma's way, and every other way, and having failed, call upon Him. Psalm 50:23 says He will demonstrate the salvation of God. He is patiently waiting for you to use up all of your "good ideas". When you finally do, He is ready and has already prepared the way through Jesus (John 14:6).

God does not discriminate (Acts 10:34). He desires all men to call upon His name (1Timothy 2:4). He is patiently waiting but His patience will not last. We will stand before Him (Romans 2:5). Don't let it be too late. Who ya gonna call?

Robbie's comments:

When a trial comes along we try to handle it every way we can and when we finally run out of time, strength, and resources we call out to God. He wants to be the first stop in our journey, not the last. Yesterday, my daughter got laid off from her job. She worked for the same company I work for and it was very difficult for me to pray.

I was very upset. She took it a whole lot better than I did. I knew I should pray and I knew I would find comfort in God but it was hard. I was confused and angry. As the day went on I kept trying to pray. My heart was heavy and I knew God wanted to take that burden off of me but His Word says that we must come to Him first. Why was that so difficult for me? Finally, I did come to Him and surrendered it to Him. Today I am much more at peace about it. I hope as the day goes on and I start feeling anxious or angry, I will go immediately to the throne of God. Don't hesitate. Whatever is troubling or burdening you, call upon God. Go to Him. He is waiting.

Jim's comments:

I am constantly calling on His name. He knows I am very needy. I really do try to take everything to Him in prayer. I have had a lot of experience doing it my way and I know that dog won't hunt.

Are You Working Out Your Own Salvation?

Philippians 2:12 (Amplified) Therefore, my dear ones, as you have always obeyed [my suggestions], so now, not only [with the enthusiasm you would show] in my presence but much more because I am absent, work out (cultivate, carry out to the goal, and fully complete) your own salvation with reverence and awe and trembling (self-distrust, with serious caution, tenderness of conscience, watchfulness against temptation, timidly shrinking from whatever might offend God and discredit the name of Christ).

The first thing I need to say is this is not about working to get your salvation. I hope by now the fact that salvation is a gift and therefore cannot be earned has been established. How something so simple and straight forward in the Bible has gotten twisted around is beyond me. I think part of it might have to do with control issues, but that is just my opinion. Anyway, Paul is telling the believer about their responsibility for their walk. The very next verse starts out "not in your own strength" so we know it is a joint effort between us and God. There are two extremes to this issue, we will explore both.

The one extreme is to think that through working out our salvation we have to do the works in order to stay saved. This view might admit salvation is a gift but we have to do certain things to remain saved. They constantly worry from day to day if they have done enough to remain in His good graces. If someone gives us a gift but we have to spend the rest of our life paying them back or they will take it back, it is not really a gift.

The other extreme is that we can do nothing ourselves. This group likes to sit around and wait for the Spirit to move them. Their lives are marked by mediocrity at best. They may have periodic movement but they usually accomplish little and they start a lot of projects but finish few. The Spirit cannot move us if we are not walking daily with Him. When we refuse to do the things necessary to stay connected we end up drifting about and being tossed around by the waves of life.

This book and our ministry are about staying connected so you can be an effective Christian. It is about balance. When most Christians talk about balance it is usually about balancing their spiritual life with the other parts of their life. That is exactly where the problem lies. Christianity is a 24/7 deal. When we talk of balance we are talking of keeping the four pillars of Acts 2:42 in balance. If we have too much Bible study we tend to get puffed up and never get out and use what we know to live a fruitful life. Too much prayer and not enough study and we won't know when God is talking to us because we won't know Him. Too much fellowship and we won't be able to help our brother because we won't have the knowledge or the prayer life to help. Too much of the Lord's Supper and it becomes nothing more than a meaningless ritual. If we keep these in balance, the Holy Spirit will have much to work with, which will result in a life that honors and glorifies God. Are you working out your own salvation?

Robbie's comments:

It amazes me every time I go to Scripture and find that we play a part in the majority of God's promises. If we do this, then He will do that. Here we have to "work out" our own salvation. Work. It takes work to live a balanced Christian life, but it is only in this balance that we find real joy and peace. Salvation is a gift, the ultimate gift, and it will result in eternity with Christ in heaven. However, our lives here on earth, need to look different than the rest of the world. Our lives should honor and glorify God. That takes work and practice and living it out every day, so that tomorrow I can do better than today, and today I can do better than yesterday. I know what it's like to put God up on a shelf and take Him down every now and then and then put Him back up on the shelf. I heard a lady once say that instead of putting God on a shelf, God put her up on the shelf and told her to stay there until she decided to become an effective Christian again. She said she stayed up there a while and then got serious about her walk, started truly working out her salvation, and only then did God take her off the shelf. If we are not being effective and allowing God to use us to change lives, we might as well just hang out on the shelf with all the other ineffective Christians. Whether you have put God on the shelf or God has put you on the shelf, let's get serious about our relationship with the Lord, and start looking radically different with a fire in our belly for Christ!

Jim's comments:

I never used to know what this verse meant. What it is talking about is getting closer and closer to God as you walk through this life. It is not working for your salvation, it's about you and God working together to make you into who He wants you to be. If all God wanted to do was wave His magic wand and we were changed, don't you think He would. We have to grow into who He wants us to be.

Are You Dead To Sin?

Romans 6:1-2 What shall we say then? Are we to continue in sin so that grace may increase? May it never be! How shall we who died to sin still live in it?

Are you dead to sin? The question isn't "Do you sin?" We all sin. This is more of a heart issue. Paul is talking about that habitual and continued sin that we are addicted to, or one we find pleasure in, and then letting it reign in our mortal bodies (vs.12). We all miss the mark and fall short from time to time. As Christians mature it should become less often and less of a pattern in our lives.

In verse 2 Paul writes "still live in it" which is as if you lived in an old run down shack and someone bought you a new house, but you decided to continue to live in the old shack. You did not just visit it every once in a while, you LIVED there. This is what he is talking about, choosing to live in the familiar, rather than the new.

In verse 6 we read that our old self was crucified with Christ and we are now no longer slaves to sin. It should not master us (vs.14). Again, it is a matter of choice. Christ is victorious over sin and death and if we are in Christ we should not let sin rule our lives. We can either live in Christ (the new house) or in sin (the old shack). This choice starts first thing in the morning. Do we turn to Him in prayer and ask for the power and guidance to get through the day? Do we look into His Word for encouragement and hope? Are we sharing our struggles with other believers? Or do we start the day on our own power and thoughts and then wonder why we haven't died to sin? We must choose either the abundant life in Christ or the mediocre life on our own. Are you dead to sin?

Robbie's comments:

The first thing in the morning... I have heard it all my Christian life about how much better it is to have your devotion, quiet time, whatever you may call it, in the morning before your day begins. I have never been a morning person. I get up in just enough time to get ready for work and out the door. While in school, I always had my quiet time at night before I went to bed. There is no rule as to when you should have your quiet time or that you even have a quiet time alone with God. But if we want to grow in our walk, that will take effort and discipline on our part. Since Jim and I started writing this book, I have discovered that early in the morning is the only time I know I can carve out of my day on a consistent basis. Right now I am sitting in bed at 5:54 in the morning writing this. Jim brings my coffee and computer to me every morning in bed so I don't even have to leave my bedroom to get my day started. I get it now. I understand how important it is to start my day off in the Word and in prayer talking to God. We are much less likely to continue living in our sin, whatever that looks like in our lives, when we start our day in the Word and in prayer. Like me, I'm sure you have heard that a lot. I would encourage you to give it a try if you are not doing it already.

Jim's comments:

I can say that there is no particular sin in which I am a slave to. I do need to watch myself when it comes to the female body. I don't know if it is my strong libido but scantly clad women sometimes draw a second glance, not a full blown stare mind you, but a second glance. This can be a problem in today's society where scantly clad woman are used to sell everything, but being d.u.I. I can keep from becoming a slave to it.

Can You Be Still?

Psalm 46:10 (NKJ) Be still, and know that I am God; I will be exalted among the nations, I will be exalted in the earth!

Can you be still? Can you sit quietly and motionless? Can you be at rest sitting silently? This is extremely hard in today's fast paced world. A world of instant messaging, microwaves, drive thru's and instant gratification. Does anyone just sit still and know that He is God?

This is an extremely important part of prayer. After the petition, supplication, intercession and thanksgiving, comes sitting still and listening to God. It means that if the mind wanders, we bring it back to focus on God and who He is. It also means to quit striving to be God or His manager. It is the ultimate stress reducer, if not eliminator. It takes practice and time but is well worth the effort.

We must remember God wants a personal relationship with us. A good relationship is two way. We speak, He listens and if we are still and listen, He will speak to us. I believe many prayers go unanswered because we won't be still long enough for Him to speak.

If we would just be still and focus on who God is in all His glory and power it would truly humble us. Be still and know He is God and know that He will be exalted and you might just start to hear His voice. As you continue this practice, it gets easier and the rewards are greater as your relationship deepens and you become an instrument of God. Can you be still?

Robbie's comments:

It did take practice for me to be still long enough for Him to speak. I was good at talking to God but not so good at listening to what He had to say to me. I find it easier when I kneel to pray or lie on my face and pray to Him. It helps me come into His presence and stay focused. It also helps to pray out loud. My mind doesn't wander and I keep my focus. Then I have to be still and listen. God does not speak audibly to me but He does give me clarity and sometimes, He speaks very clearly to my spirit. When I was at the end of my rope with Jim, He spoke very clearly to me by telling me to "get out of His way"; to surrender it all to Him and quit trying to fix Jim. When I got out of God's way, it allowed Him to fully take control and it was almost immediately that I started seeing God at work in Jim's life.

Jim's comments:

No! Next question! Seriously though, I do have a problem sitting still and listening. I continually want to be doing something. I find it hard to sit in church without tapping my foot or something. I think I have ADHDTV or whatever they call it. I think my parents just said I was antsy. I do try to listen to God and that is why when I go for a walk or a run I don't take headphones so I can listen to Him.

Can You Forgive?

Ephesians 4:32 Be kind to one another, tender-hearted, forgiving each other, just as God in Christ also has forgiven you.

Do you find it difficult to forgive those who have offended and/or hurt you? You know those people that every time they walk into the room you tense up and start to think unpleasant thoughts. Those people who just rub you the wrong way. Those people who annoy you by their very presence. Those people who you think are the problem when it is really you.

What you are feeling is resentment. Resentment is ill will or anger caused by a sense of injury. Did you notice it says "sense" of injury? They may not even know they have offended you. Either way, we are to forgive them. To forgive means to cease to feel resentment. We are to forgive just as we have been forgiven by God.

Not only does the Word tell us to forgive others, but medical studies have shown that deeply held resentments cause all sorts of physical ailments. Not having a forgiveness that comes from the heart is like you drinking poison supposing that the one who hurt you will be injured. The one who has offended you probably sleeps quite well at night. You are giving him rent free space in your head that will continually take away your joy and give the enemy ample ammunition to keep you from being effective for the Kingdom. We are to have clean hands and a pure heart, (Psalm 24:4). Holding resentment "heart" or plotting revenge "hands" is neither. The easiest way to start the forgiving process is to pray. Pray for them and then pray for your self to be like Christ and forgive completely.

We are to forgive others, not just for our sake, but also for theirs. 2 Corinthians 2:7 states we are to forgive others or they might be overwhelmed with sorrow. What a testimony it would be to non-believers if we Christians would tell those who have offended or hurt us that we forgive them. Forgiveness is the number one Christ like characteristic. That is why He came, that is why He died, and that is why we are forgiven.

Forgiveness is not being a door mat. We are not to stay in an abusive relationship continually forgiving those who abuse us. God gave us a heart and a brain. It is also easier to forgive once you have removed yourself from the situation. Please do not confuse forgiveness with giving someone the right to abuse you. Seek outside help whenever necessary. Can you forgive?

Robbie's comments:

About 20 years ago, one of my best friends from college called me to tell me she was getting married. I was so excited for her. She started telling me all the plans for the wedding and who was going to be in the wedding party. Guess what? I wasn't one of them. She was going to have about 8 bridesmaids and I wasn't one of them. I was shocked and deeply hurt. I was bitter about that for years. I know that sounds petty but the hurt was real. You see, it's not only the common, obvious things that can hurt us and make us bitter; it can be the little day to day things also. I finally did forgive her but it took years. I am sure she never had any idea that I was hurt. I never said a word. It was quite a relief when I could finally let that go. Forgiveness gives us freedom to move on. It can be hard and it might take time, but it is worth it.

Jim's comments:

Can I forgive someone? All my life I have been able to do this and I believe it is because I have done so much harm to others and they have forgiven me that I usually don't hold a grudge. God has just made me a very forgiving person.

Are You Too Busy Building Your House?

Haggai 1:4 (Amplified) Is it time for you yourselves to dwell in your paneled houses while this house [of the Lord] lies in ruins?

Are you so busy building your life that you have set your relationship with God off to the side? In the book of Haggai, he explains what happens when the people's personal affairs interfere with God's business. Verse 6 illustrates how circumstances become difficult when we put our own interest before our relationship with the Father. Your labor is no longer blessed by Him. You earn wages to be put into a purse with holes in it. That sounds an awful lot like debt.

There are many things we can put first before God. Our children are one. Do we go to Sunday morning athletic events because it will help their athletic careers? What we are really saying is getting ahead is more important than being in God's house. A stand for God is more important than one meet or game. If we truly believe God and His Word, we will look for much but it comes too little (vs.9).

There are many other situations that get in our way, such as our toys. Do we say "I'll give more once I have my stuff. I will serve more once I've climbed that corporate ladder. I will spend more time with God when I am not so busy with life."? Excuses lead to a path far from God where it is easier to justify what we want and not what He wants.

Don't be like the people Haggai preached to, dwelling in their nice homes (paneled houses) while God's house lay in ruins. Be about the things of God first. Seek His face and His will and all this will be added to you. Put down your toys and go up to the mountain. Bring wood and rebuild the temple that He may be pleased and glorified (vs.8). Are you too busy building **your** house?

Robbie's comments:

Busy. That seems to be the plague of today's society. I also believe it to be true. Sometimes it is used as an excuse for everything and sometimes it is true. We are just too busy. We have busied God right out of our lives. I know when I put so many other things before Him as a priority, and use busy as an excuse, it is just wrong. Plain and simple. That is why I think it is vital to keep everything in balance and keep your relationship with God as the number one priority. I think it is more difficult to make God a priority when you are a young couple with small children. It is very difficult to find time for everything and unfortunately, it is usually our relationship with God that suffers most. I beg you to stay "daily under His influence". Seek Him first and everything else will fall into place.

Jim's comments:

I used to be too busy for God but just like this passage, all came to nothing. I try hard every single day to put Him first in everything I do. I have learned from experience it will not work any other way. Even in the ministry we can crowd God out by being so busy doing "His" work all of the sudden we look around and say "Where's God?".

Do You Love The World?

1 John 2:15 Do not love the world nor the things in the world. If anyone loves the world; the love of the Father is not in him.

Do you love the world? Not mother earth or the people on it. The definition of "the world" here is how the lost operate. Its characteristics are pride and covetousness. It is the system of self first. It is best exampled in today's advertisements. You deserve it... you owe it to yourself... this product is a must have to be somebody or to get that person you desire. It's lust, not love, it's money over relationships, and "I'm going to get mine... to heck with everybody else". It's loving things and using people.

There is nothing wrong with new cars, nice clothes, fine restaurants, or first rate vacations. If you are a good steward and can afford all of those, that's great. On the other hand, if you work so much that you sacrifice time with your family to get what you desire then that is "the world". If you hold back giving just so you can "get" that's "the world". If your relationships are just with people who can advance your agenda, that's "the world". If you will do **anything** to get ahead, that's "the world". When you hoard, that's "the world". The world is what Satan offered Jesus (Matthew 4:8).

Does your world view come from the Bible or TV? Are you under constant pressure to "keep up with the Joneses"? Do you always have to have more and better, no matter what the cost? Do you have real friends or just associates? Is your confidence in Christ or things? Do you love the world?

Robbie's comments:

I have to admit I do love some things of the world. I like nice things. I struggle with being a good steward of my time and money. I'm thankful I don't have a competitive spirit. I'm not about keeping up with the Joneses or wanting more or better. I have noticed that when I am a good steward of my time and money, God blesses me. My goal is to be about God's business and not the world's business.

The only way I can do that is by working at it daily. I have to remind myself daily. I have to read my Bible daily. I'm definitely not there yet, but I'm trying.

Jim's comments:

I do struggle with the fact that I like "things". Nice cars, houses, vacations, and the like. I try to keep balanced and go to Him for all my wants. Again, there is nothing wrong with nice things, just don't acquire them the world's way. Put Him first and let Him decide what you should have.

Had A Spanking Lately?

Hebrews 12:8-9 But if you are without discipline, of which all have become partakers, then you are illegitimate children and not sons. Furthermore, we had earthly fathers to discipline us, and we respected them; shall we not much rather be subject to the Father of spirits, and live?

Who likes discipline? I remember as a child I sure didn't. But as the old saying goes "The older I get the smarter my parents get". I may not have enjoyed the discipline but it was for my own good. Sometimes what I received was punishment, meant for pain. Discipline, while it can be painful, is more about correction than pain. Discipline is usually only painful after the softer warnings were ignored. I once heard it said "Pay attention when God whispers, you do not want Him to raise His voice".

Have you ever seen children out in public who you knew by their actions that discipline was lacking in their home? Have you seen parents try to reason with a toddler? Trust me, God is not that way. He loves us too much to let us wander to where we might get hurt. He is also too holy to let us who call on His name damage that name by our actions.

If there are certain areas of your life that are not pleasing to God and you continue those behaviors without regret or consequences, the writer of Hebrews claims you are illegitimate. It would be wise to check your salvation to be sure you are a son or daughter.

God's discipline can be a gentle nudge such as a feeling of discontentment when you pray, that constant dilemma that pops into your mind until you rectify the situation. If you continually ignore it He will have to raise your awareness level. If He has to He will make a public spectacle of you. We have all seen Christian leaders publicly fall because they ignored His warnings. They may have tried to hide an alcohol or drug addiction only to get a D.U.I. or drug bust. They may have tried to hide a passion for the ladies only to get caught in a prostitution sting, an affair, or with pornography. Pay attention when God whispers.

Look closely at every area of your life. Where is God whispering? You will not like it when He YELLS!!!!! Had a spanking lately?

Robbie's comments:

I've raised my children to believe that they are never too old for a spanking as long as they are living under my roof. I was raised with spankings and I raised my children with spankings also. Children's personalities are very different. It's amazing how different even twins can be. My daughter, Corrie, always wanted to please and spankings were not the proper discipline for her. She was usually very sorry for whatever she had done. Her twin sister, Casey, on the other hand was very defiant and not so remorseful of her actions. Sorry she got caught, oh yes, but not sorry for what she had done. Spankings were a little more common with her. I wanted her to know that we would not tolerate her behavior and sometimes a spanking was what we thought was the most appropriate consequence. Jamie, my youngest, was somewhere in the middle. I know there are some of you who don't believe in spanking your children. All I can tell you is it worked for me when I was growing up and it worked for my children. It makes us think twice before we do that behavior again. We understood that we were being punished for disobedience. It's the same with God. He may not physically reach down and spank us, but He lets us know that we have been disobedient, and He disciplines us in a way that will get our attention so that we will think twice before doing it again. Just like Casey, Corrie, and Jamie, God gets our attention and disciplines His children differently. The point is, He does discipline. We discipline our children because we love them. God disciplines us because of how much He loves us also. He loves us more than we can ever imagine. I don't like my "spiritual spankings" but I know they are done out of love for me and for that I am truly thankful.

Jim's comments:

I have had God beat the hide off of me. Even after I came to Christ I still struggled with drugs and alcohol. It wasn't so much the using as the outright lying that He would discipline me for. I would think I had everybody fooled and then He would cause it all to come crashing down in a very painful way. He will not be mocked by His children.

Conclusion

Do you know, that you know, that you know, that you are forgiven? Forgiveness is the key to Christianity. We could not come before a Holy God unless we were clean. In the Old Testament before the priest could come into the Holy of Holies, which was in the presence of God, he first had to offer sacrifices for his sins. Once he was clean, he could enter and atone for the nation as a whole. That is why the veil to the Holy of Holies was torn when Christ died. We are now clean and can come into His presence. I have seen Christians, who have not completely understood the totality of God's forgiveness, live in defeat because Satan uses that guilt to keep them paralyzed. We are completely forgiven and we need to live like it.

Once we know we are completely forgiven we should live in obedience to the One who set us free. Forgiveness is not a license to sin and as we just read, those He loves He disciplines. Once we realize we have been forgiven, then we can forgive others. If we continually call out to Him, and then be still enough to listen, He will speak to us. Of course we can't be too busy building our own house or loving the world or we won't be able to hear Him. Being different and not just acting differently is what Christianity is all about. Our prayer is that as you keep reading, God will speak and you will let Him change you. Let's do ten more.

Chapter Eight

Mountain Moving Faith?

Do You Please God?

Hebrews 11:6 And without faith it is impossible to please Him, for he who comes to God must believe that He is and that He is a rewarder of those who seek Him.

It has been said "He who loses money loses much, he who loses a friend loses more, but he who loses faith loses all". How is your faith? Is it lost, misplaced, or your strong tower?

The dictionary defines faith as "a firm and earnest belief, trust, reliance on the statements, strength or qualities of another". As Hebrews 11:6 clearly states, it is impossible to please God without it.

Let's look at some Biblical faith. Enoch, one of only two humans mentioned in the Bible to go directly to heaven without dying, was taken up by faith (Hebrews 11:5). Genesis 5:22 of the Amplified states "Enoch walked (in habitual fellowship) with God". The connection here is in order to have faith you must be in habitual fellowship with God. Not just Sundays, some days, or special occasions, but everyday.

Taking the definition above, do you have a firm and earnest belief in who Jesus is, that he was born of a virgin, died on a cross for our sins, was physically resurrected, and ascended into heaven to sit at the right hand of the Father? Do you place your trust in Him? Do you believe ALL His statements (the Bible)? Do you rely on His strength and not yours? Do you live in His qualities of peace, love and joy? These are just some of the rewards of those who seek Him. Do you please God?

Robbie's comments:

The Bible teaches us that all are given a measure of faith. I believe it is our responsibility to grow that faith. How do you measure faith? Hebrews tells us that faith is being sure of what we hope for and certain of what we do not see. We have faith in the air we breathe. We do not see it but we are sure it is there. Are there times you wonder if God is really there? When our faith is strong, we are sure He is there even though we cannot see Him working. I think we have all been through times in our lives when it appeared that God was nowhere to be found. In our heads we know He is there because His Word says He will never leave us, but in our hearts we doubt. It is during those times of doubt that I have to get flat on my face and cry out to Him. We don't always understand God's timing and His ways and we never will. That is when our faith must be strongest. One of the strongest examples of faith in the Bible for me is when Abraham was willing to sacrifice his son, Isaac, by faith and obedience. Wow. I believe our faith is tested in some way every day whether big or small. Keep growing your faith.

Jim's comments:

My faith is the only thing I have. I base my existence on it. I operate my life on it. I base my eternity on it. It is the only thing that is real to me. Friends and family may disappoint me and possessions may be taken from me, but my faith will see me through.

Who Are You Listening To?

Psalm 1:1 How blessed is the man who does not walk in the counsel of the wicked, nor stand in the path of sinners, nor sit in the seat of scoffers!

Have you ever gotten bad advice from someone? Have you ever taken your own advice and wished you hadn't. This whole Psalm is about rejecting worldly advice and accepting God's advice. If you listen to God's advice, you will be blessed. The word "blessed" means happy, fortunate, prosperous and enviable. The opposite would be sad, unfortunate, poor, and pitiful. Who are you listening to?

I am not saying that unless someone is a Christian you should not listen to their advice. There are non-Christians that actually give godly advice. There are principles in the Bible that worldly people follow because they make good sense. Just in a financial sense, there is saving, giving, working hard, being subordinate to your employer and being fair in your dealings with customers. All of these are principles found in the Bible and they are useful to anyone who uses them. There are success seminars everyday in this country and these seminars are run by non-believers and presented to non-believers. They are using principles straight from God's Word and people are putting them into practice to become successful.

This Psalm is more about being grounded in God's Word (vs.2) so you will know what kind of advice you are being given. We as Christians have His Word and the Spirit to discern the advice from others. The problem is we live in a culture where the line between good and evil is constantly being moved or removed all together.

When this Psalm talks about the wicked they are talking about those that are disobedient and living apart from God. They have no standard on which to apply their advice. This is how a pregnant woman can be counseled to do the "right thing" and have an abortion. This is how we can be persuaded to go into debt and get that "thing" that we deserve. This is how we get convinced to vote for someone who will take from those who have and give it to those who don't. This is how two people of the same sex can be united together and call it marriage. This is how our country has gotten into the moral decay of today.

We must use the Word, the Holy Spirit, other believers and prayer to discern the advice we are given. Not the media, politicians, or celebrities. The church should be different and not be plagued by the moral decay around us. Divorce, abortion, debt, and pornography should not have the same statistics in the church as in the world. Who are you listening to?

Robbie's comments:

It is so sad, yet so true, that the church doesn't look much different than the world today. We hardly even blink an eye anymore when we hear about a Christian couple getting a divorce or a Christian business man who has no integrity in his business practice. I believe we have gotten too complacent and too silent. We have sat around and watched the moral decay of society and then wondered how we got here. We have listened to the enemy long enough. He has convinced us that we can't make a difference and that our opinions don't matter. There is great power in numbers but numbers start with the number one; one person, one idea, one cause. The irony is that when we start to stand firm and take a stance we find others that are like minded. We need to quit listening to others who think we are crazy for being a little radical. We need more radical Christians. What are you passionate about? God has put that passion in your heart for a reason. Listen to Him. Ask Him what you are supposed to do with that passion. If it's of God others will climb on board. Get radical!

Jim's comments:

I check everything against the Bible. Even those I trust and admire, I check what they say against the Bible. When I do ask for advice or receive counsel I make sure their walk matches their talk. I would not take financial advice from someone who can't pay their bills nor would I take dieting advice from someone overweight. If a person giving the advice won't follow their own, why should I listen to them?

What Are You Looking At?

Hebrews 12:1-2 Therefore, since we have so great a cloud of witnesses surrounding us, let us also lay aside every encumbrance and the sin which so easily entangles us, and let us run with endurance the race that is set before us, fixing our eyes on Jesus, the author and perfecter of faith, who for the joy set before Him endured the cross, despising the shame, and has sat down at the right hand of the throne of God.

I would like everyone to pay attention to what you are looking at for just one day. Is it people, TV, your possessions, stock market, bank account, internet, or worse? Do your eyes stayed fixed on your problems? What are you seeing as your day goes by? Are you like the saints before us keeping your eyes on God?

Hebrews chapter 11 is called the great hall of faith because it lists the great people of faith in the Old Testament who kept their focus on God and His promises, including the coming Messiah. Abel brought a better sacrifice than Cain and died for it. Noah saved his family and mankind. Abraham was about to kill his son. Sarah had a baby after she was too old. All these died without seeing the promise. Faith and their eyes set on God brought them through.

We are living the promise if we keep our eyes on Jesus and His work on the cross. The reason we cannot lay aside every obstacle and hindrance is that we keep our focus on our obstacles and hindrances. Auto racers are told not to look at the wall because where your eyes look, you are apt to follow. Turn your problems and your hurts over to Christ. Keep your attention on Him and you will run the race with patience and power.

Are you focusing on the problem or the solution? The problem entangles, but the solution is Jesus. What are you looking at?

Robbie's comments:

I was studying the book of Hebrews one time and we were on the faith chapter, Hebrews 11. We went through each verse and talked in detail about the faith that was demonstrated by each example; by faith

Abel..., by faith Enoch..., by faith Noah..., by faith Abraham...,
and on and on we went just marveling in the miracles God can and
wants to perform in our lives if only we would have enough faith.
The last verse in the chapter is verse 40. My teacher made us write
in our Bible a verse 41 and it started with, by faith (and we inserted
our own name)...., So mine said by faith Robbie.... Wow! Did that
make me stop and think? What great and mighty miracle(s) would I
or could I write that God has done in my life as a direct result of my
faith? It really made me stop and think. If you were to add verse 41
to Hebrews 11 what would your statement be?

Jim's comments:

I sometimes can get easily distracted. If I did not keep my daily
five prayer list with me I would probably not pray much throughout
the day. If I did not study the Bible every day I am sure I would
eventually just open it on Sundays in church. I need to keep my
eyes and my focus on Jesus or I would just drift along living a very
mediocre life.

Are You An Encourager?

Hebrews 10:24-25 And let us consider how to stimulate one another to love and good deeds, not forsaking our own assembling together, as is the habit of some, but encouraging one another; and all the more as you see the day drawing near.

Are you a cheerleader, cheering on your fellow brothers and sisters in Christ? Or are you an Eeyore? You know the type that is so negative when they walk in the room they suck all the joy out of everybody. Those who are so displeased and unexcited about their walk they can't see anything positive in those around them. Those people who, when you feel God leading you to do something big, only tell you all the reasons why it can't be done.

In these verses, the writer is telling us to think about how to excite others to action. We need to give people the encouragement to go ahead with the God-sized task that He has given them. We should rally around each other with positive prayer and Scripture cheering each other on to victory. Satan, the flesh, and the world, are our enemies. We do not need other believers to add road blocks and detours. One reason so many Christians fail to live the abundant life is fellow believers telling them they can't or shouldn't.

I encourage you to be an encourager. Pray to stay positive and lift up those around you. I hope you are not neglecting the assembling together because when you do it is so negative. When you gather together, lift up the name of Jesus and encourage each other and live out the abundant life. Are you an encourager?

Robbie's comments:

I really would like to think that I am an encourager. I try. I hope the people I know are not reading this and laughing because they don't see me as an encourager. I want people to dream big, to go for what they feel God calling them to do no matter what the rest of the world might say or think.

I know that there were some who thought Jim and I were nuts when we started d.u.I. ministries. Jim left a good job but knew God was calling him. The economy was struggling and he was leaving a regular paycheck for no paycheck at all. As a matter of fact as I am writing this, the ministry has just become "official" and we have not raised any money yet for the ministry. With that said, however, we have a group of prayer partners who have been praying with us and for us now for about four months and have done nothing but encourage us as we step out in faith to see where God will take us and the ministry. I am so thankful for my prayer partners! I think it is so important to encourage and to be encouraged. That's why I love being around my brothers and sisters in Christ. They are my family. Please continue to encourage one another.

Jim's comments:

I do love to encourage. I am a very optimistic person. I always try to see the good in everybody and in every situation. I enjoy coming along side someone and helping them go further than they think they can.

Are You Worse Than An Unbeliever?

1 Timothy 5:8 But if anyone does not provide for his own, and especially for those of his household, he has denied the faith and is worse than an unbeliever.

Do you take care of your family? Back when Paul wrote this it was directed at the men who were the bread winners of the household. Today, the situation is vastly different, but God's Word remains the same. If you are a man, it is your obligation to take care of your family. If your wife can make more than you, and you want to be a stay at home dad, you still need to be the head of the household and the spiritual leader.

Any children that men father should at the very least be aided financially by them regardless if they live under their roof. It is the man's responsibility, not the state's, not the mother's. God's Word is very clear on this. A man of faith should show the fruit of his faith by providing for his own.

We, as Christians, cannot yield to the growing appetite of the government to take over our children's life. We need to be financially responsible for our children. We need them to understand our world view from a Biblical standpoint. If the men don't take care of their children, who will? Are you worse than an unbeliever?

Robbie's comments:

It was very difficult taking on some of the roles as the head of the household while Jim was drinking. We still went to church every Sunday, but going to church on Sunday mornings does not make you the spiritual leader in your home. Jim was making good money (when he was working) but blowing most of it and then of course, we couldn't pay our bills. It is absolutely vital for the man to take the role as head of his household seriously. When I look around at the destruction and dysfunction in families today, there is usually one common theme and that is the husband is not the godly head of the household God commands him to be. If you are a single mother then you must take on this role. God will help you. He is faithful.

Surround yourself with good Christian friends and families. Whether father or single mother, it's a huge responsibility. Take it seriously. God does.

Jim's comments:

I was worse than an unbeliever. When I was active in my addictions I absolutely did not take care of my family. If it wasn't for other family members helping out we would have lost way more than we did. I am much better at it now, especially the non-tangibles, like love, spiritual leadership and counsel.

Do You Call Evil Good?

Isaiah 5:20 Woe to those who call evil good, and good evil; Who substitute darkness for light and light for darkness; Who substitute bitter for sweet and sweet for bitter!

In our world today up is down, black is white, and evil is called good. Just pick up any newspaper or turn on the TV and see what the world now calls "good". Abortion is choice, homosexuality is an alternate lifestyle and adultery is what everybody does. As I write this, the governor of New York was caught in a high price prostitution sting. I actually heard a news commentator say "this would go by unnoticed if he was just having an affair with a consenting adult". Up is down, black is white, evil is called good.

As Christians, we have a clear definition of what is "good". Not only do we have His Word written down, we also have the Holy Spirit to guide us and prompt us to do good. When we try to excuse away what we know to be evil by saying "everyone else does it", "it's really not that bad", or "other people are worse", it's just a short trip to calling evil, good.

When abortion was first legalized the proponents said they wanted it to be safe and rare. It is neither today. It is certainly not safe for the baby or for the mothers' mental health, spiritual health and now, we are finding out, physical health. Gays, at first, just wanted to not be ostracized. Now, they want to be married and their lifestyle called normal. Unwed mothers were sent away to have their babies. Now they are celebrated as single moms. The list goes on and on. We would much rather save an owl or tree than a baby.

We, as Christians, need to not get caught up in this trap. We need to stand on God's Word and call evil what it is. God's rules are not to diminish our fun. They are for our own good if not for our own survival. Just look at this country's statistics and see if normalizing bad behavior has been good. You really don't need to look at statistics, just look around. Do you call evil good?

Robbie's comments:

It sickens me to look around and see how far we have drifted from our Biblical principals when it comes to so many issues in today's society. If we would unite as one we could take back some of the things that we have sat back and watched get taken away from us. We can't have "Christmas" programs anymore in the schools. There are far more people who celebrate Christmas than not. So why did we sit back and let good become evil and evil become good? We need to find our voice and fight for what we believe to be true, honorable, just, pure, lovely and commendable (Philippians 4:8). There is strength in prayer and in numbers!

Jim's comments:

I am a black and white kind of guy. There is no gray area. Those who think there is usually have very little gray matter. Just kidding, but I do believe the Bible is very clear on most issues that matter and that is where I take my stand.

Are You Asking For A Calf?

Exodus 32:1 Now when the people saw that Moses delayed to come down from the mountain, the people assembled about Aaron and said to him, Come, make us a god who will go before us; as for this Moses, the man who brought us up from the land of Egypt, we do not know what has become of him.

Do you get impatient waiting on God? Did you forget the God who brought you to where you are today? I don't know if your deliverance was as dramatic as the Israelites exodus from Egypt but as quickly as they turned, we can too. The main reason for their turning away was impatience. Moses delayed and they completely turned to another god. The worse part of it was that they were getting something better... tablets written by the finger of God. (Exodus 31:18).

How is your patience while waiting on God? Are you willing to wait for God's best or are you turning to a calf (vs.4)? It takes a disciplined prayer life to wait on God. Through our prayers we communicate our needs and desires (Philippians 4:6). It is through prayer and meditation (listening) we wait for God's timing. He knows and wants what is best for us. Prayer, meditation, and Bible study are crucial for aligning ourselves with His desire for us. We cannot simply pray once and assume He will answer in the next 24 hours. Patience and discipline are two characteristics of a person being used by God.

What are the calves in your life? What old character traits do you fall back on when it seems God is not listening? Where do you go for advice when you are unclear about a decision? What do you do with your money to try and make things happen? Do you have the patience and discipline to wait on God's best or are you asking someone to make you a calf? Are you asking for a calf?

Robbie's comments:

Sometimes, it is so easy to give up on a dream or start doubting whether God has even heard our prayers. We are a society of instant gratification and God sometimes says "not now". We must persevere and not give up. I know many of you can relate to me when I say that there are certain things in our lives that we pray almost every day for, yet God has still not answered our prayer as we would like. All I can say is don't give up. Keep praying and then pray some more. I prayed for Jim's sobriety for years and years. I knew deep down that God heard my prayers and I couldn't give up. Frustrating? Oh yeah. Confusing? You bet. But I knew that it was not God's will for Jim to be an alcoholic and destroy his life and the lives of those around him, so I just kept praying. To be honest, it was the only thing I could do. There were days I doubted I would ever see him clean and sober but I couldn't stay there long, I had to get back to hope and prayer. Remain faithful in prayer and don't give up.

Jim's comments:

I was very impatient but I am getting better. I have learned to wait on God. I don't like to wait but I am learning how to wait. The key for me is to be busy doing something else while I am waiting. Learning God has what's best in store for me makes waiting a little easier.

Are You A Ham?

1 Chronicles 4:40 They found rich and good pasture, and the land was broad and quiet and peaceful; for those who lived there formerly were Hamites.

This verse is kind of like the prayer of Jabez. 1 Chronicles 4:24-32 is listing the descendants of Simeon. He was the second son of Jacob and Leah. As the author is recording their names and where they journeyed to, he stops to reveal this little gem. The place they went to settle was found to be in excellent condition because of who was there previously. The Hebrew actually reads "the people of Ham had dwelt there of old and left it a better place for those who came after them."

So, are you a Ham? When you leave a situation or place is it better than when you arrived? When you enter a room, are people glad to see you or glad to see you go? Are people better or bitter after you leave them? When shopping, do you put your cart back, and when you realize you don't want a product, do you just put it anywhere? When you borrow something and return it does it look as good as, or better than, when you received it?

These are just some of the little things we could do to make life better for others. In everything we do, we should be making life better for those who come behind us. Are we going to leave behind a better world? Are we going to leave behind a world where the Gospel can still be preached? Are you Ham?

Robbie's comments:

I don't remember where or when in my Christian journey I started thinking about some of these concepts.... putting the shopping cart back, putting the product back after I decided I didn't want it, but it happened. All of a sudden I became grossly aware of these things. Maybe it was after I worked at a department store part time one Christmas season and spent most of my time putting away clothes that people left in the dressing rooms. Sometimes they didn't even bother putting the clothes back on the hangers, just leaving them inside out lying on the bench. For non-Christians, I would expect this type of behavior but if you are a believer and still do these types of things, I would challenge you to think twice next time. As Christians, we should be trying to be part of the solution and not part of the problem. Go the extra mile. Be men and women of integrity. Don't only put your cart back but take someone else's cart back with yours. People are watching and God is always watching. Be a Ham!

Jim's comments:

I am a Ham. I hate seeing products left just anywhere in a store because people are too lazy to put them back. Most everything I do I like to see if it can be done better or faster. I love improvement. As I write this I am not bringing in any income, therefore I can't tithe to my church. Instead, I make breakfast for our Sunday school classes. I always try to help make peoples' experiences pleasurable.

What Have You Done With Your Talent?

Matthew 25:14-18 For it is just like a man about to go on a journey, who called his own slaves and entrusted his possessions to them, To one he gave five talents, to another, two, and to another, one, each according to his own ability; and he went on his journey. Immediately the one who had received the five talents went and traded with them, and gained five more talents. In the same manner the one who had received the two talents gained two more. But he who received the one talent went away, and dug a hole in the ground and hid his master's money.

When these verses talk of talents it means a sum of money. We can talk about the money God has blessed us with, or the abilities, or just the 24 hours in a day. This parable is about what we have done with what He has given us.

I hear so many people say "If I only had that person's money, or that person's ability, or more time I would…" The truth is the richest man doesn't have enough money or the poorest enough time to do all that needs to be done. Time and money are both commodities of which we need to be good stewards. When we throw in our talents and abilities we see the need to do the most with what we have been given.

In this parable we see that each was given according to their ability. That is why five made five more, two made two more, and so on. Whether you are a five, a two, or a one you still have to use what you have wisely. When you use your money wisely, more will be given to you. Using your time wisely will result in more and better opportunities. If you are asking for more without using what you have effectively, I doubt you will get it. Why would God want to see you waste more money and opportunities? To each that has more will be given.

You can begin right now with your time. Use it wisely. Stay balanced in what you do. When you work, work hard. When you worship, do it from the heart, joyfully. When you play, have a good time. When you sow, expect to reap. Whatever you do, do it to the best of your ability. Get the most out of your time, talents, and money and God will say "Well done good and faithful servant". What have you done with you talent?

Robbie's comments:

When I ask myself "what have I done with my talent", I have to first ask myself "what is or are my talent(s)?" I don't have any natural abilities that just stand out. I can't sing, I can't play an instrument, I am average at best at any sport I attempt to play, and I don't have a creative bone in my body. I do believe I have the gift of giving. I love to see others get blessed by God. I give whenever and wherever I can. The problem with that is, I don't have a lot to give either but I give what I can in hopes that God will be honored. It is very true, that I must first be thankful and manage what God has given me, before He is going to bless me with more. I heard it once asked about someone who wanted a bigger house, "are you being a good steward of the house you have now?" If you want more money, are you being a good steward of the money you have now? If your excuse for anything is that you are too busy, are you being a good steward of the time you have now? That's a big one for me because we all know we find time for the things we want to do and think are important in our lives. I quit saying "too busy" years ago because the fact of the matter is, if I think it is important, I will find the time to do it. I want to use my talent for God. I want my motives to always be pure and true. I want to be blessed with more because I have been a good steward of what God has given me. I know you do too. Let's go out and use what God has blessed us with today.

Jim's comments:

I try to do the most with what I have. I get ridiculed at my house for putting small amounts of stuff back in the pantry or fridge. I hate seeing anything go to waste. I hate throwing anything away because you never know when you might need it. Every time I see a penny on the ground I will stop and pick it up. Just yesterday, I was at Tim and Robin's house helping him and Lorne move Tim's cousin,

Annette, into their basement, and there were all these pennies on the floor. I had to force myself to not stop and pick them up. I am trying to apply this to the talents and gifts God has given me also.

How Is Your Joy?

John 15:11 These things I have spoken to you so that My joy may be in you, and that your joy may be made full.

How is your joy? Not how happy are you. Not how excited are you. How is your joy? The dictionary defines joy as: the state of being very glad, pleased, great delight, gladness of heart. Joy is internal and based on Christ. Happiness is external and based on circumstances. Joy is something no one can take from you. No situation can remove it either. It is the peace that surpasses all understanding and Jesus wants your joy to be made full!

How do we get this joy? We start by the words spoken in verses 1-10. Jesus is the vine and we are the branches. We must stay connected to Him in order for the Vinedresser (The Father) to prune us. This pruning is done through difficult circumstances. That is why James tells us to count it all joy (James 1:2). If in a difficult circumstance, we pull away from Jesus, the Father can't work in us and we lose our joy. Anytime we move away from God we lose our joy. For our joy to be made full, we have to let God prune us. Then we will bear much fruit. Anyone with a fruitful walk is full of joy.

There is also joy in obedience. Hebrews 12:2 talks of the cross as the joy set before Christ. That joy comes in believing what God says, then doing it, no matter what the cost. Could you ever see being crucified as the joy set before you?

There is joy in prayer. Paul speaks of offering prayers with joy when praying for others (Philippians 1:4). What a joy it is to intercede for others. To go before the throne of grace for someone else and then watch that person's life be changed by God is truly a joyous occasion.

There is joy in singing. Psalm 67 reads, "Let the nations be glad and sing for joy". Your praise and worship should be full of joy. A joyful heart cannot help but sing. Sing loud and sing to Him. The joy of singing comes from the heart, not the voice box. If you have lost your joy, get reconnected. Whenever there is distance between a believer and God, we know who moved. How is your joy?

Robbie's comments:

It is so true that joy is not a feeling. Joy is a state of being, not an emotion. It comes from within. We all know that sense of joy and peace when we are connected to God and feel close to Him. I love worship music. One of the times I am most joyful is when I am singing praises to God. (It may not sound too joyful to others, but to God it is a joyful noise!) I can just lose myself in worship music. Music can touch the depths of my soul like nothing else and I experience true joy, that gladness of heart. I have heard some of my brothers and sisters say that worship music just doesn't do anything for them and that we have to be careful not to get lost in the emotion. I say they are missing a true blessing by not allowing themselves to surrender to the words and music and depth of true worship through music. Sometimes I just like to close my eyes and pray the words of a worship song. We can stay connected to God and remain joyful through many things. Pick what works best for you. Don't allow anyone to steal your joy. They can't do it without your permission. Stay connected and remain joyful.

Jim's comments:

My joy is okay. It might not be full because I still let in too much of the world. I sometimes gage my success by the world's standards instead of God's. I really try to keep things simple and let God worry about the results, and let my joy come from Him and not what others think or say.

Conclusion

Faith is the foundation of Christianity. Faith that God is good helps us weather the storms of life. Faith that heaven is real eases the pain of death. Sometimes faith is all we have. A strong faith will keep you from asking for a calf. It will fill you with joy. It will help you use your talent to the fullest. Be careful who you listen to so as not to let others diminish your faith. We pray this book will help strengthen your faith.

Do you encourage people or are you the negative type who finds fault in everything and everybody? Do you leave people bitter or better? Do you take care of your family to the best of your ability? Are you careful of what you are watching so you know the difference between good and evil? The world is watching and they want to see if we Christians really believe what we say. If that belief is not seen in our actions, they will know it, and then question our faith. Do we really believe?

Chapter Nine

What Is Your Dream?

Where Are Your Roots?

Colossians 2:6-7 Therefore as you have received Christ Jesus the Lord, so walk in Him, having been firmly rooted and now being built up in Him and established in your faith, just as you were instructed, and overflowing with gratitude.

As I read the Bible, there are times I wish I would have taken a course in agriculture. There are so many illustrations such as "sowing and reaping", "vine and vinedresser", "harvest", "seeds", "winepress", "gleaning", and so on. These examples were used because everyone would have understood the writer. Today, not so much.

I will attempt to shed some agricultural light on these verses. First, the root is what firmly attaches the plant to the soil so that it remains stable. It is also how that plant is furnished nourishment and sometimes where plant food is stored. Another definition of root is "source or origin" and rooted is defined as "being firmly established".

Paul is instilling in his readers the fact that we must be firmly attached to Christ to withstand the effects of the world. Christ is also where we get our nourishment through His Word. Being attached is also how our food is stored, by being able to call up the Word when we need it. Being rooted in Christ Jesus keeps us firmly established in the faith.

Are you rooted? Are you being built up in Him? Are you established in your faith so as when you walk people see Him? Are you overflowing with gratitude that He is your nourishment? Where are your roots?

Robbie's comments:

The more I read the Bible the more I realize the huge responsibility we have as brothers and sisters in Christ. There is a lot of work to be done for the Kingdom while we are here on earth. When we think of that statement many times we think about evangelism, but not all of us are called to be evangelists. We are to share the Gospel with others when prompted by the Holy Spirit, but we should be obedient to the Holy Spirit no matter what He is calling us to do. The only way to know what the Holy Spirit is prompting us to do or say is to be in constant fellowship with Him. It sounds so cliché but it's just a fact. I need to work on being able to call up the Word when I need it. I need to be in constant prayer with Him all through my day. I need to fellowship with other believers and I need to be in a Bible study learning from others like you. If you want to live a faith filled, grounded by the root, and firmly established Christian walk, you need all these things too.

Jim's comments:

My roots are deep in Christ. Because of my past and having tried to live my life my way and the results being so devastating, I finally came to the end of me and Christ was all I had. I know for sure if I do not stay rooted in Christ I am doomed and will drift along in mediocrity or worse.

What Are You Talking About?

2 Timothy 2:15-16 Be diligent to present yourself approved to God as a workman who does not need to be ashamed, accurately handling the word of truth. But avoid worldly and empty chatter, for it will lead to further ungodliness.

What do you talk about on a daily basis? If you recorded yourself and played it back each night, what would be your reaction? Would you be ashamed? Would it be mostly empty chatter? Or, do you speak the truth in love? Do you handle the Word accurately when wrongheaded theology is tossed around?

I know this a difficult task. James 3:8 tells us that no man can tame the tongue. We have to be slow to speak and think our thoughts through. The Holy Spirit finds it difficult to work if we will not shut up long enough to listen to Him. Also, what we put into our head is what will eventually come out. If we fill our heads with worldly ideas and fleshly visions that is what will be coming out of our mouths.

We must know the Word and study it continually. We must let the Word transform our minds on a daily basis. We must have the right material in us for the Holy Spirit to work. He can't cause you to call up something that is not there. As believers we should know what we believe so we will not be ashamed to defend our faith or to share it. Pay attention to what comes out of your mouth because those around you are. What are you talking about?

Robbie's comments:

Ok, God must really be trying to tell me something here because these are the exact same verses we just got through discussing last night at Bible Study. I was convicted then and I am still convicted today. I find a little bit of comfort in the fact that we all struggle with taming the tongue. We all say things we shouldn't and I knew when this was going to be the topic for the week in Bible study, I was in trouble. It's like a diet, the more you think about it the more you want to eat. Well, the more I tried to tame my tongue the more I got frustrated and lashed out saying things I shouldn't. This happens mostly at work. I have got to be determined and strive for no ill word coming out of my mouth. It's a process and a learned behavior. It takes discipline and being more in the presence of God and less in the fleshly, worldly nature. It is so true that others around you are watching. I hope I do better today than yesterday. That's what d.u.I. is all about, learning how to live a life that glorifies God, one day at a time.

Jim's comments:

I try to keep all talk wholesome but when a bunch of guys get together and we start to cross a line it's all down hill from there. Once we slide past where we know we shouldn't, it is hard to get it back. I try to be diligent about this but sometimes I am weak. It is another area that I need to continue to work on.

Do You Have A Dream?

Genesis 37:5 Then Joseph had a dream, and when he told it to his brothers, they hated him even more.

Do you have a dream? A God inspired, God sized vision in your head that you believe God wants you to achieve? When you tell people your dream do they try and squash it? Do they tell you how many ways it can't be done? They may even think you are a little loco. If you have a dream and it is God inspired, you have but one choice and that is to pursue it.

I believe we were all created for a purpose and your dream is your purpose. Your passion is your purpose. All you have to do is bring your dream and your obedience to God together and it will happen. God has a purpose for you and it is something you like to do. The only way to know it is to be d.u.I. and be in His word and let it speak to you about your dream. Much prayer and fellowship with others, and getting their feedback, and giving and serving at a local church, will open the door of opportunity for your dream.

Stay away from dream stealers. Those who are negative and continue to tell you "it" can't be done. This may come from other believers who figure if God is not working in their lives surely He can't be working in yours. Joseph's brothers are a perfect example. Joseph, through faith and obedience, lived out his dream. It was uncomfortable at times and so may your path to fulfilling your dream. Remain faithful and steer clear of naysayers while staying connected to God and listening to His voice, the voice of Truth. Do you have a dream?

Robbie's comments:

I had to be taught how to dream. I had to be taught that it was OK to dream. If we believe we serve a big God that loves us beyond measure, why are we so afraid to come to Him with our goals and dreams? If we are grounded in our faith and walking daily with Him, then our dreams will want to please Him and honor Him and show others just how real God is. I see so many Christians today who think there is something wrong with wanting God to bless us. What they don't realize is that God wants to bless us and He wants to bless us in big ways! We are His children and He loves us. If our dreams and goals line up with His Word and you believe that God is still in the blessing business, then don't be afraid to dream. As a parent, don't we want to bless our children? Not spoil them and give them everything they want, but if you knew their true heart's desire and were able to give that to them, wouldn't you? I sure would, and I know that if our hearts are right and our desires are pure, then God wants to bless us with our heart's desire. But, if we don't believe He will, then He probably won't. I believe God blesses us in proportion to how much we desire and believe that God is still in the blessing business. I am believing God for some pretty big things in my life that I know only God can accomplish. I hope I never stop believing God for big things in my life and I hope you don't either.

Jim's comments:

I am a dreamer, always have been and always will be. Since I finally got right with God the dreams have gone from being fantasies to actual God given dreams that will come true. I have always dreamed big and expected them to come true. You are reading one of my dreams and d.u.I. ministries is another. God and I are not finished yet.

Have You Answered "Here I am"?

1Samuel 3:4 That the LORD called Samuel; and he said, "Here I am."

Has God ever called out your name? Have you had that unmistakable call to do a God size task? Did you say "here I am"? Or did you say "who me"? Or did you pretend you did not hear him?

Here Samuel is called and he believes it to be his master, Eli. Just the same, like a good servant, he gets up immediately and answers "here I am". He does not yell from his room "what do you want?" He is a loyal and trustworthy servant. Even after the second and third time he goes in and answers "here I am". Do you respond that way?

God sometimes calls us through others asking us for our help. Are you in tune enough with the Holy Spirit to jump up and say "here I am"? Will you put aside self and what you want to do to be able to do what He desires? Listen closely when you are prompted to do something God-sized. Be alert to that still small voice urging you to come up higher.

If you are going to listen to God and serve Him, it pays to have a godly mentor. Eli knew God was calling Samuel and bypassing his family because of his son's sins (vs.13). Eli did not get in the way or try to lead Samuel astray even though God's word to Samuel was devastating to Eli and his family. Eli did what was right and allowed the anointing to pass to Samuel and he answered "here I am". To what will you say "here I am"?

Robbie's comments:

I think we don't see God-sized miracles much anymore because we don't really believe God is in that business anymore. God is still God and I can't find anywhere in Scripture that says He is going to get out of the God-sized task business. I know He has worked a God-sized task in my life. He has made my husband a whole new creature. I would say He has given me my husband back but what He has given me is far better. We cannot possibly hear what God is saying or asking of us if we are not in tune to His will for our lives. That requires being daily under His Influence. We want to hear from God and we want those God-sized tasks and miracles in our lives, but are we willing to quickly respond "here I am"? To get everything God wants for us it will take work and time on our part. The question for me is not "here I am" but "am I willing"? Let's be willing today to seek God first and do whatever we feel God prompting us to do or say.

Jim's comments:

I try to be obedient when He calls and usually I am, the problem sometimes is being too busy to hear the call. I get on my own agenda doing God things and get tunnel vision and sometimes I miss His call when it's right in front of me. Even when He called me to full time ministry I, like Gideon, set the fleece out twice to be sure.

Are You Looking Back?

Genesis 19:26 But his wife, from behind him, looked back, and she became a pillar of salt.

Are you driving down the highway of life with your eyes firmly fixed on the rear view mirror? Are you constantly looking into your past at all the disappointments and hurt? Or, are you looking into the past at all your victories and continually reliving them? Either one will get you into trouble. We need to focus on Christ and what He is doing in the present.

Lot and his family were told in verse 17 not to look back. His wife looked back anyway and paid the price. Did she look back because she was leaving the familiar and no matter how bad that was, she feared she would miss it? Surely she had friends there and was worried about them. Maybe she was afraid of starting over someplace new. The point is she was told not to look back. She was told where to go and how to get there. When God speaks, whether through angels, others, or directly to us, we must obey and not look back at what He has told us to leave.

The problem with continually looking at your past is you cannot see what God has for you in the present. Satan will keep bringing up past sins and hurt. You will begin to say "if only" or "what might have been". Satan will also bring up our past to keep us distracted from doing anything in the present. When looking back our flesh can sometimes rose-color what we thought were the good times of our old life. If we are paralyzed by our past then we are not effective in the Kingdom.

An occasional look into the past is healthy. It allows us to see our growth. We can see past mistakes and not make them again. We must not dwell on our past but use it as a tool and a testimony. Focus on God and what he wants you to do today. We are to be the salt of the earth, not pillars of salt. Are you looking back?

Robbie's comments:

I once heard it said "you cannot change your past, but you can make your past part of your ministry". What a great way to take a not-so-great past or set of circumstances and use them for God's glory. God brought you through it for a reason. What Satan meant for destruction, God can use for good. Whenever I look back I am amazed at where God has brought Jim and me. I won't lie. It was tough but the blessings on the other side are beyond comprehension. Persevere and don't give up. God loves you and can use whatever circumstances you have been through to grow you and prepare you for your "ministry".

Jim's comments:

I used to look back and wish I could change the past because I screwed up so badly. I heard it said once in A.A. that you can change your past by doing the right thing today, because if you live right today eventually it will be your past. Now I look back to the past as a marker to see growth or areas where I need to improve. The past is a tool for a better tomorrow.

Are You Jealous?

James 3:16 For where jealousy and selfish ambition exist, there is disorder and every evil thing.

Isn't it appropriate that James uses the words "jealousy" and "selfish" in the same verse? Jealousy is one of the highest forms of selfishness. Jealousy says you shouldn't have that, I should. Jealousy says you shouldn't be happy, I should. Jealousy says why is God blessing you when He should be blessing me. Jealousy looks all around and says they shouldn't but I should.

James is so right when he writes, where jealousy and selfish ambition exist, there is disorder and every evil thing. Disorder is a direct result of selfish ambition. If everyone on a project wants to be the one in charge, nothing gets done. If a group is not united in their purpose, nothing gets done. If a Christian is so jealous of what others have been blessed with, there will be no joy in their walk or unity in their church. Jealousy cries out "ME" while unity humbly says "we".

A spirit of jealousy keeps the individual in bondage and keeps the church from its purpose. It is always looking at what others have and we don't. Once jealousy rears its ugly head, it will spread throughout the church. It starts with a few who say, "God, we follow Your Word, we do the right things, why have You blessed others and not us?" Jealousy looks to find faults in others so as to keep us from examining ourselves and correcting our own faults. Once it begins to spread, the focus on Him is lost as we focus on self and why we don't have what others have. It is a deadly cycle and needs to stop immediately.

The sure fire way to stop jealousy is to rejoice when others are blessed. Continue to look at what you have and not what you lack. Pray for others to be blessed. Take your eyes off yourself and your wants and look at how to help others. At the first sign of jealousy from others put a halt to it. It will spread. Keep the focus on Him and His power and glory. Be thankful in everything. Are you jealous?

Robbie's comments:

I was watching a movie and heard a girl say, "I would just like to be able to pay the rent, the utility and the phone bill all in the same month". Been there! I have to admit that there are other people that have things that I would love to have. Do I begrudge them for having these things? Absolutely not. Good for them. I just pray they are using it as God would have them to use it. I believe God gives us abundance to enjoy and to share. I am grateful for everything I have.

Jim's comments:

I am not the jealous type. My wife has never given me reason to be jealous and if I see something someone else has I figure if they can get it, so can I. I really am content with what God has blessed me with and what He will bless me with in the future.

Do You Pursue Peace?

Romans 14:19 So then we pursue the things which make for peace and the building up of one another.

What do you pursue? Money, things, attention, love, respect, the opposite sex, or God? We can and do strive after many things, but what is number one on your list? As usual, if number one is the right one, everything else on your list will fall into place.

How do we pursue peace? How is life free from disturbance and agitation achieved? The beginning is to seek God's face the first thing each day. Unload your burdens to Him. Ask for guidance to keep your eyes off self and to look around to those who He has placed in your presence for you to help. Ask Him for your provisions for that day. Stay attentive to His voice as He guides you through the day. Be willing to be stretched by the Holy Spirit. When an uneasy feeling or situation arises, go to Him in prayer immediately. How many times has something small gotten blown out of proportion because we did not stop and pray to keep it in perspective?

Another way to pursue peace is to not be consumed with what others around you do. All of Romans 14 is about using your freedom wisely and not judging your brothers. Most of our strife in life is from perceived slights by others or us trying to run everyone else's life. If a brother or sister does not do it your way, and is not sinning, don't worry about it. Keep your focus on harmony and being d.u.I. God can, and will, guide us through every predicament if we ask Him and then let Him. Do you pursue peace?

Robbie's comments:

There are many life lessons I have learned through recovery. One of the biggest lessons for me was to realize that the only person I can change is me. I was so busy trying to fix Jim that I didn't realize that not only could I not fix him, but I needed to be working on me, trying to correct some of the control issues and pride I found in myself. I will never forget the freedom and peace I felt the day that I finally and completely surrendered it all to God. Real peace can only be found in God. We have to seek Him and pursue Him. It has to be a constant in our lives not just hit or miss if we want that peace that surpasses all understanding. The closer we are to Him the more peaceful our lives will be. Perfect? No. Peaceful? Without question.

Jim's comments:

I am a very peaceful person. I pursue peace almost to a fault by not wanting to make waves even when they are needed. I enjoy peaceful and harmonious relationships where strife is at a minimum. I do try to seek Him in everything I do so as to keep situations peaceful and stress free.

Are You Merciful?

Luke 6:36 Be merciful, just as your Father is merciful.

Are you compassionate, sympathetic, tender and responsive? That is what merciful means. It sounds like the characteristics of a little old lady. You know the one; she reads her Bible daily, always has a smile and volunteers for everything. The truth is every Christian is to be merciful.

We will start with compassionate. Do you have feelings for the troubles of others? Sometimes we say they got what they deserved. Other times, we will lecture them on how they shouldn't have gotten into that situation. What we need to be is like Christ. Feel for their troubles and ask what we can do to help. We cannot criticize without love or without offering a solution.

Next is sympathetic. Sympathetic is to be affected by the feelings of others. This may not require a solution, just a hug or to sit and listen. It is the ability to sense when someone else is down and then decide to just be there for them.

I am sure most men would love to skip over tender, but again, it is what Christians are to be. To be tender is to be sensitive, expressive of the gentler emotions. We are to use kind words, bright cheerful outlooks and no harsh tones when helping others with their problems. It is to be loving, kind, and gentle.

The fourth characteristic is responsive. We need to be responding readily. Not saying we need to go pray about it, not saying someone else will help, or saying "that's not my gift". Being merciful is being ready to respond whenever the situation arises. That is why we need to be d.u.I. We have to be ready at all times and that comes from being controlled by the Spirit. Remember, our Father is merciful to us, so we must be to others. Are you merciful?

Robbie's comments:

What jumps out at me when I read this is under "sympathetic" when it says "then decide to be there for them". We know as Christians we are to have these characteristics but let's be honest, sometimes we just don't feel like it. When it isn't the natural response, we must then "decide" to be these things. That is why living the abundant Christian life is a daily walk and many times, daily work. The only way to grow is to work at it. It won't come by doing nothing. Salvation will get you to heaven but if you want to tap into the many blessings God has in store for you here on earth, then you must do your part. Paul is continually telling us to stop acting a certain way and start acting another way. Why? Because he knows where the blessings are... God has them. But, we will never find them if we are following flesh and not the Holy Spirit. Be merciful today even if you don't feel like it. God will bless your efforts and before you know it, it will be your natural response.

Jim's comments:

I am not merciful and to pass it off as being a "man thing" is wrong. Some of it goes back to my past and not getting too close to people because I did not want them to see the real me. The longer and deeper my walk with Christ, the more He breaks my heart for people. If you ask me in another year I would say there will be a considerable improvement.

Are You Thankful?

Ephesians 5:20 (Amplified) At all times and for everything giving thanks in the name of our Lord Jesus Christ to God the Father.

Do you express gratitude for favors received? Do you genuinely give thanks for all you have? Do you realize everything you have is from God? Even your very existence. Paul says to give thanks at all times and for everything. Is that how you live your life?

Just think how the world would be changed if everyone would say these two simple words, "thank you". No matter how little the task we said "thank you". No matter how else it was compensated, we said "thank you." When our spouse or our children did something we said "thank you". When we start and end our prayers, we said "thank you".

As believers we have a gift to really be thankful for - a new life in Christ now, plus eternity with Him in heaven. We must thank Him for the little things, not just the big. Thank Him for the morning, the rain, the sun, the pain, the joy, the food, the friends, the job, etc. etc. This type of thankfulness comes from the heart. It springs from a life that has truly been changed and realizes that God is everything and we are nothing. That is true humility.

We cannot go through our life just nodding our head and murmuring "thanks". We must look people in the eye, smile and say a big "Thank you!" Not only will it change those around us, it will change us. Living a thankful life is a great witness. Are you thankful?

Robbie's comments:

Wow! Am I thankful? I am thankful for so much. I would encourage anyone who is struggling or trying to find their way back to God to start by just listing the things you have to be thankful for. When times are tough and struggles are upon us, it's easy to get caught up in the negative and discouragement. We can't get bogged down in negativity, although it is easy to do. We must concentrate on the things we are thankful for. I have to admit that I was never thankful for a struggle or devastating circumstance. However, I can say that in the midst of it I could always find something to be thankful for. There is always someone going through something worse. To this day, I have to stay away from negative people. I can so easily get caught up in it and before I know it I am saying and thinking negative things. God is good and I have found on the days I walk with Him, not only are the negative thoughts fewer but the thankfulness multiplies.

Jim's comments:

I am very thankful because I know it all comes from Him. The fact that I owe my very existence to Him makes me thankful. Now, do I act that way all the time? No. That is why on my prayer list of five that I carry with me daily is a reminder. In the lower right corner of my list is how many days of sobriety I have. When I pray the list I start with "Thank You Father for 1,192 days of sobriety…" or, however many I have on that particular day. There are days when I get all fleshy and forget it all comes from Him but that does not last long before He shows me the error of my ways.

Are You Double-Minded?

James 1:8 Being a double-minded man, unstable in all his ways.

Are you double-minded? Do you operate on faith or feelings? Do you ask God and then not wait for the answer? Do you allow others to sway you from your convictions? Do you even have convictions? As Christians we have the stability of God's Word to keep us from being blown to and fro by the winds of what is new today. It is the anchor that holds in the storm.

We also have the Holy Spirit to guide us. Through prayer and meditation we can let God set us on the path He wants for us. This path may not be the easiest, but it is the best. We can also counsel with other Christians to make sure we are hearing God. Be careful to make sure those others are walking the walk. We must be slow to speak and quick to listen. We must also be careful of making decisions based on emotions.

We, as Christians, have everything we need for a stable life - a God who loves us, Christ who died for us, the Holy Spirit who guides us, other believers who encourage us, a church that revives us, and a future that is glorious. Are you double-minded?

Robbie's comments:

I don't think I am double-minded. I am very firm in my convictions and don't sway much to and fro. My friend, Angie, told me she was spending time in prayer and just kept claiming God's truths. She would shout out "Truth!" and then recite a verse of Scripture such as Jeremiah 29:11 "For I know the plans that I have for you, declares the LORD, plans for welfare and not for calamity to give you a future and a hope".

"Truth!" "For our struggle is not against flesh and blood, but against the rulers, against the powers, against the world forces of this darkness, against the spiritual forces of wickedness in the heavenly places". We can only find stability in God.

Jim's comments:

As I stated before I am a very black and white kind of guy and my convictions are based on the truths of the Bible. The times that I might waver on something are when my will and His are not on the same page but it usually does not take long for me to yield.

Conclusion

Well, do you have a dream? Surely God has given you a passion for something. In order to figure out what your dream is you must stay rooted in Christ. If you know what your dream is you need to stay rooted in Christ to fulfill it. Is what you're talking about contributing to the dream or taking you farther from it? Have you answered "here I am" to begin the journey to your dream. Once we start this journey we cannot keep looking back longing for the familiar, no matter how hard it gets. We can't be jealous of other's dreams or be double-minded about our own. If we pursue peace, be merciful, and are thankful for everything, our path along the way will be much smoother. Our dream is that believers would take their walk and their relationship seriously and somehow this book and d.u.I. ministries would play a small part. Let's go to the last eleven.

Chapter Ten

Finally, The Last Eleven!

How Often Do You Remember?

Luke 22:19 And when He had taken some bread and given thanks, He broke it and gave it to them, saying, "This is My body which is given for you; do this in remembrance of Me".

How often do you partake of the Lord's Supper? Is it once a week, once a month, only on holy days, or just randomly? Is it only when your church offers it? When you do partake of it, why are you doing it? Are you just doing it because everyone else is? Do you feel you have to? Is it your part of the salvation package that you must do in order to stay saved? Let's look at what the Bible has to say about the Lord's Supper.

When Christ first offered this to the disciples it was during the Passover meal. The Jews held the Passover in remembrance of the Exodus out of Egypt. God leading them out of Egypt and out of bondage was a foreshadowing of Christ dying on the cross to lead us out of bondage to sin. Just as the Jews had their Passover lamb, we have ours in Christ. Both had to be slain to gain freedom. Just as the Jews have their Passover in remembrance of what God did for them we, as Christians, have our Lord's Supper in remembrance of what

He did for us. Just as the Jews were led out of Egypt to serve God (Exodus 7:16) we are set free from sin to serve Him.

Now that we know a little about it, when should we do it and how should we do it? The Bible really doesn't set any certain times or regulations. It appears they did it every Lord's day or every time they had a meeting. I think this gives us plenty of latitude. We must remember WHY we are doing it. In the verse above Christ says "Do this in remembrance of Me". He doesn't say in remembrance of what He did on the cross. He says in remembrance of Him. This could mean His whole life. The fact He left heaven and came here to live as a man and be humiliated. He suffered abuse at the hands of those He came to save when He could have called down a legion of angels or just destroyed them with a word. Partaking of the Lord's Supper is to think about ALL He did for us and how, at times, we really take it for granted. Let me offer some suggestions for making this event more meaningful.

The decision of when to partake of the Lord's Supper is up to the individual believer. I do it when it is offered at my church. I do it at home when I am alone. I do it whenever I feel the need to remember what He has done for me. When life is really clicking, I need to stop and remember why it's clicking and Who is behind it. When things get a little tough, I need to stop and remember how tough He had it. If I slip into mediocrity, I need to remember what He did and my need to serve Him with excellence. There is the trap of doing it so often it becomes meaningless. Avoid this by being led by the Spirit in all your service. Mix it up in the way you do it. Watch a clip from *The Passion of The Christ* just before partaking of it. Do it right after a spiritual inventory. Do it with your mate or family. The main thing is do it in remembrance of Him.

There are some churches where it does become meaningless. They do it so on schedule, some people come in, go through the line, then immediately go right back out the door. It has become nothing more than a ritual to be checked off of their list. The Lord's Supper is one of the four foundational requirements for a powerful Christian walk found in Acts 2:42. Prayer, Bible study, and fellowship are the other three. Prayer and the Lord's Supper are the most under-utilized in many Christians' walk.

There are guidelines for the spirit in which you take the Lord's Supper. They are found in 1 Corinthians 11:23-34. Verse 28 tells us to thoroughly examine ourselves before we eat of the bread and drink of the cup. Some people misinterpret this by refusing the bread and cup saying they feel that because of something in their life they are unworthy to partake. We are all unworthy, that is why He came. We are to examine why we are taking part in it and fully realize what He did. Verse 30 tells us that careless and unworthy participation is why many are sick or have died. I believe this is a good reason to examine our motives and be sure of why we are doing it. I say do it as often as the Spirit leads and with a lot of prayer because we as humans are quick to forget and slow to remember the goodness of our God. How often do you remember?

Robbie's comments:

I have to admit that I am one of those that only partook of the Lord's Supper when offered at church. I never even thought about taking it at home or anywhere else. That sounded sort of sacrilegious to me. I thought it had to be done in a formal setting. That's because I have only ever seen it done in a formal setting or service. Again, the Bible only says to do it in remembrance of Him. It doesn't matter what you use, what kind of juice or wine, what kind of bread or wafer. A few weeks ago I was really having a big time pity party. I got to work and felt really awful and convicted about how I was acting. I had so much to be thankful for and needed to remember the love and sacrifice of Jesus. I got to work and really felt the desire to have the Lord's Supper, to remember and honor Him and get out of "self". All I had were Fritos and grape juice! I sat at my desk and partook of the Lord's Supper with my Fritos and grape juice. I'm sure some of you are saying "that's not the Lord's Supper, that's just a snack!" I believe God is looking for what is in our hearts, not what is in our hands.

I would encourage you all to get alone with God in the next day or so and have the Lord's Supper. It might seem a little weird at first but I think you will be blessed and realize just how much and how often we need to remember Him. You can do it anytime, anywhere. Even with Fritos!

Jim's comments:

This is something that has been a recent development in my walk. As I studied the Bible and how the early church got its start, God began to show me its importance. I prayed over the situation and now I do it quite regularly because I want to call to remembrance all He has done for me.

Want To Stay Out Of Trouble?

Proverbs 21:23 (Amplified) He who guards his mouth and his tongue keeps himself from troubles.

There is an old saying "better to keep your mouth shut and let others think you are a fool then to open it and remove all doubt"! That is sort of what this proverb means. How many times have you thought "I wish I wouldn't have said that"? I have seen couples hurt each other more deeply with words than fists. The scars from words last far longer than physical ones. Most physical altercations start with words. It is true; he who guards his mouth and his tongue keeps himself from troubles.

James says no man can tame the tongue. So how do we guard our mouths? One way is to pray for our enemies. It is hard to say something negative about someone when you are praying for them. If you want what is best for those around you, how can you speak evil of them or to them? Maintain a positive attitude through the words you speak.

Another way is to think before you speak. This takes practice. James 1:19 says we are to be quick to listen, slow to speak and slow to anger. If we spend more time listening and processing what is being said, it allows the person we are communicating with to feel that their opinions matter. If we are formulating our comeback while they are talking, we are not really listening. Everyone likes to be heard. If we slow down, we can see where the other fellow is coming from and respond properly.

Another way our mouth gets us into trouble is by saying "yes" too much. We say "yes" when we really don't want to, which causes us to do the task with resentment. We say "yes" when we really know we can't so we end up disappointing others. We also say "yes" when it is not what God wants us to do. He has something better which we will not get to do. Again, quick to listen and slow to speak. Think, process, and pray before answering.

The language we use also gets us into trouble. Cussing and sexual innuendos can ruin a testimony quicker than you think. This type of talk has no place in a Christian's life. I know it can be a hard habit to break, but God can and wants to remove it from you. We need to apologize when it slips out and continually pray to have Him remove this nasty habit. If you have a real problem with your mouth, check your heart. Jesus says out of the abundance of the heart the mouth speaks (Matthew 12:34). Want to stay out of trouble?

Robbie's comments:

When I was a little girl, my mouth got me into far more trouble than my actions. It's no different for me today. I know you have heard it said to "speak your mind". I think the more accurate statement here would be "speak your heart". It is so true that we speak our hearts more than our minds. When I am angry, my words are sharp and cutting; my voice is loud and shows my heart of anger. When I am happy, my words are more loving and kind. That is my heart speaking, not my head. Our dog, Buffy, leaves the room when either Jim or I raise our voice. Sometimes, we don't even realize it and then all of a sudden, we see her leaving the room. She is our "voice control" monitor. I will actually lower my voice and check my heart when I see her leaving. It makes me realize that God is right there in the room with me also and doesn't like it anymore than Buffy does. I have to learn to control my tongue and let nothing come out of my mouth that isn't glorifying to God. That is easier said than done so I'll just keep trying.

Jim's comments:

I try and guard my mouth but sometimes I speak faster than I can think and it gets me in trouble. The key here is for me to be quick to listen and slow to speak. My problem is I can hardly wait to give someone my opinion whether they ask for it or not. I need to be guided more by the Spirit and less by my emotions.

Are You Fooled By The Shell?

1 Samuel 16:7 But the LORD said to Samuel, "Do not look at his appearance or at the height of his stature, because I have rejected him; for God sees not as man sees, for man looks at the outward appearance, but the LORD looks at the heart".

How many times have you been disappointed by someone because you judged them by their appearance? How many times have you been pleasantly surprised by someone you originally over-looked on account of their appearance? Either way, the old saying is true "you can't judge a book by its cover".

God's Word tells us not to judge others (Matthew 7:1). But, in John 7:24 it tells us to be honest in our judgment, not according to appearances. In Matthew 7:1 the judging is critical and condemning. John 7:24 is judging honestly, not superficially. It is a fair and righteous judgment. It is looking at more than one aspect of someone. It is about knowing them and their heart.

We have to judge people. If not, we could easily get caught up in the wrong crowd. We could quickly be led astray if we did not consider one's actions and true beliefs. It takes time to know someone's heart and we must be cautious until we do. Cults start by people blindly following someone they haven't had time to judge by God's Word or standards.

We also judge people by their looks and/or what they have. We can sometimes be fooled by people appearing to be successful, only to realize their only success is in acquiring things. We, in America today, are caught up in what one has and therefore, what they can do for us. There is nothing wrong with those who have, but we shouldn't base our relationships on what they have or what they can do for us.

We also pass over those that appear less fortunate. We don't want to get our hands dirty or be involved with someone that is needy. Again, we look at what they can or in this case, can't do for us. How many lasting friendships are we passing up because people don't appear to meet our standards?

If we truly want to be like Christ, we need to observe people at the heart level, getting to know them and seeing if their actions and their words line up. We need to come along side others, regardless of how they look, and get involved in their lives and see how we can help. That is what Christianity is all about; spreading God's healing one relationship at a time. Are you fooled by the shell?

Robbie's comments:

Instead of shell I like the word "mask". I wore a mask for years not wanting others to know what was going on in my life. I was dying on the inside but didn't even know it. I just wanted to lock myself in a room and hide but that would bring attention to me and I didn't want to say or do anything to bring attention to myself. I didn't want others to know what a mess my life really was. Taking off that mask was one of the most freeing moments in my life.

Jim's comments:

I have been pleasantly surprised by some people but mostly I am disappointed when I judge by the outer shell. I am learning God's way and just accept people the way they are and not get caught up in appearances. God looks at the heart and that is what I need to do also.

Are You A Whisperer?

Luke 12:3 Accordingly, whatever you have said in the dark will be heard in the light, and what you have whispered in the inner rooms will be proclaimed upon the housetops.

Ben Franklin was right when he said "three people can keep a secret, if two of them are dead". That is basically what Jesus is saying here. Whatever you whisper will be proclaimed. How many times has something you said in confidence been repeated to others? How many times have you broken someone's trust and repeated what you should not have? Regardless if the statements are true or false, if we don't want others to know what we have said, we probably should not be saying it.

There are times when conversations should be kept in confidence. Still, during that time, we should never say anything about somebody that we wouldn't say to their face. Frank discussions about others and their troubles should be about how we can help. They should not be about how bad they are, how far they have fallen, or how far we expect them to fall. All discussions should be about helping bring towards repentance and back into the fellowship. Here prayer is absolutely essential.

Talking about others and not knowing if it is true, talking without helping find a solution, or stating something you know is not true is all gossip and rumor. This is the worst kind of whispering. It has no place in a Christian's life. If you are doing it, stop. If you are around others and it starts, either stop it or walk away. Everybody struggles with something. We need to be about building up and not tearing down. This is where being guided by the Spirit is most important. Words hurt. Remember, if you can't say anything nice, say nothing at all. Are you a whisperer?

Robbie's comments:

Sometimes I think women are born with a "gossip" gene. It's just so natural, so second nature... so very wrong. It serves no purpose and edifies no one. I have come a long way in this area. I am by no means where I need to be but praise God I am not where I use to be. I still find myself sometimes right in the middle of talking about somebody. I know when the words are coming out of my mouth that I shouldn't be doing it and then I beat myself up afterwards and ask myself "why did I engage in that conversation?" "Why did I say those things?" I normally don't start the conversation but does that really matter?

I can say that I very rarely believe what people say about other people. I have to hear it from the source itself before I put any credibility to it. I have been fooled too many times by things others have said that have either been taken out of context or way over-exaggerated. Don't believe everything you hear. I am praying that I will concentrate on being part of the solution instead of part of the problem.

Jim's comments:

I never really had a problem with this since I became a believer. In my previous life, oh yeah. I actually have kept secrets that others thought I had shared and I had just cause to reveal them, but did not. If I hear gossip I try to stop it.

What Are You Dwelling On?

Philippians 4:8 Finally, brethren, whatever is true, whatever is honorable, whatever is right, whatever is pure, whatever is lovely, whatever is of good repute, if there is any excellence and if anything worthy of praise, dwell on these things.

What are you dwelling on? The definition of the phrase "dwell on" is to say or think about much, to hold to. Whatever thoughts dominate your day, or whatever you talk about much, is what you are dwelling on.

Do you dwell on things you cannot change? That's why I love the Serenity Prayer, accept what we can't change, courage to change what we can and wisdom to know the difference. If there is something that cannot be changed like the death of a loved one, go to the cross and leave it there and rest in God's peace and love. If it is something God can change and you can't, bathe it in prayer. If it is something you can change, ask Him for the power to carry it out.

Do you dwell on things you shouldn't? The list here is as long as our sinful nature can make it. If you find yourself talking of things you shouldn't or thinking things you shouldn't, you again go to the One who has the power to remove the stronghold from your life. You must take every thought captive. Better still is to fill your head with God's Word and encouragement from other believers. You must be careful of what you think and say because eventually you will act it out.

Do you dwell on the "what ifs" and "if onlys"? If that is the case, then you are saying one of two things… either you are not being obedient to God's direction for your life, or worse yet, He doesn't know what is best for your life. The remedy for this is prayer, God's Word, and being around other believers. This allows the Holy Spirit to guide your every step.

Paul gives us a good list of what to dwell on. Whatever is true, honorable, right, pure, lovely, good repute, excellent and worthy of praise. Basically, dwell on God, His Truths and His love. What are you dwelling on?

Robbie's comments:

This is one of the first verses I memorized. I think it was because it was one I needed the most to remember! I can get very passionate about things, and when I do, I tend to dwell on what I can't do anything about anyway. Recently, Jim and I had seen and heard others talk about a few things in the church. Nothing big, just some changes that other people would like to see or frustrations they felt. However, it sounded more like complaining then trying to find a solution to a problem. Jim and I are trying to be more proactive and less reactive so we came up with a list of things we had seen and heard and gave it to our Elders. We called it Comments, Concerns, and Suggestions. We gave it with no expectation. We are trying to dwell on the good and if we see an issue or problem, address it. There are so many things to be thankful for each and every day. Let's take every thought captive today and dwell only on those things that are good, true, noble, right and honorable.

Jim's comments:

I always try to keep the conversation on a positive note. I focus on the solution not the problem. I hate being around people who, if they won the lottery would complain about paying the taxes. Life is too short, we need to remember the Serenity Prayer "accept the things we cannot change, change the things we can, and the wisdom to know the difference".

Is Your "Yes" Yes?

Matthew 5:37 (Amplified) Let your Yes be simply Yes, and your No be simply No; anything more than that comes from the evil one.

When you tell people "yes" do they believe you? When you tell them "no" do they try to change your mind? Do you often try to explain your "yes" or "no"? Do you have to swear on your mother's grave? Do you follow every "yes" with "I promise this time"? When asked to do something do you say "I'll pray about it" then walk away and never think of it again? If any of these scenarios describes you, you need to simply let your "yes" be yes and your "no" be no.

This verse is kind of like the double minded man in James but there is a difference. The double-minded man drifts back and forth in his answers. Here what we are talking about is knowing how you really want to answer but not doing so. It is more about saying what you think people want to hear than answering truthfully. We, as Christians, need to be people of our word. We need to speak with integrity and authority. We need to under promise and over deliver. There is nothing wrong with saying "no" if you can't get to it. And there is everything wrong with saying "yes" to everybody because they make you feel guilty. We should always yield to the Spirit. That is why staying d.u.I. is so important.

The verses right above these is talking about the commandment "do not take the Lord's name in vain" which a lot of people think only refers to cussing. That is a part of it, but it mostly means "I swear to God" when making a statement. The Hebrew actually means "lightly" or "frivolously", in false affirmations, or profusely. There are many Christians who wouldn't think of using God's name profanely but casually say "I swear to God" when stretching the truth.

We just need to be people of integrity. We shouldn't try to please people with our speech. Speak truthfully and boldly and let people know that they can count on what we say. If we say we will do something, do it. If we say we can't, it should be because we can't, not that we don't want to. Is your "yes" yes?

Robbie's comments:

   This was a hard one for me to learn. I used to be a people pleaser and I'm sure many of you feel the same way. I would tell people I would be somewhere or do something and then not follow through. I was afraid of being honest and just saying "no". The funny thing is people would much rather hear the truth, than hear what you think they want to hear and then be disappointed when you don't follow through. For me it was a maturity issue. With maturity came boldness for me. I often tell a person now that "no" is a complete sentence. The key is to be in tune to what you feel the Holy Spirit guiding you to do or say. Sometimes we need to do things we don't want to do and should say "yes" when we really want to say "no". We also need to be aware of over committing and burn out and learn to say "no" when you might really want to say "yes". It's all about balance and following the Holy Spirit. We should all be men and women of honesty and integrity.

Jim's comments:

   I sometimes have a little difficulty with this one. I wrote before about being a people pleaser and that is what this is talking about. Wanting to say "no" but saying "yes". The only thing I can do is continue to pray and ask God to remove this character defect. If I tell you "yes" I will do it, it might be grudgingly, but I will do it. Again I need to be guided by the Spirit, not the flesh.

Do You Have The Gift Of God?

Ephesians 2:8-9 For by grace you have been saved through faith; and that not of yourselves, it is the gift of God; not as a result of works, so that no one may boast.

Who doesn't like getting gifts? Did you ever receive a gift from someone for no reason at all? It wasn't your birthday, not an anniversary, not Christmas, and it wasn't a thank you for something you had done. It was just a gift. This gift wasn't just a pair of socks either. It was the best gift you had ever received. And you not only didn't deserve it, you were hostile to the One giving it. That is the Gift of God.

Paul is stating that grace is a gift from God. This gift cannot be earned no matter what we do. Once we receive it, it cannot be taken away no matter how bad we fail. It does come with one string attached. To get the most out of this gift, we must put self aside and make God number one in our life. He also gives us another gift to help us get out of self. That gift is the Great Comforter, the Holy Spirit.

All we need to receive this awesome gift is faith. Faith in Who Jesus is, faith in what Jesus did, and faith in what Jesus said. Just reading through the Bible you can see this gift being offered over and over again, but most won't receive it. I suppose there are as many reasons why they won't receive it as there are people.

One reason is that some believe they are good people. They don't see themselves as needing a Savior. Others think they can work their way to salvation. The problem then arises how much work, and if I mess up, do I need more. Some may even think they are too awful for salvation. Not so! We are all the same. The main sin is turning from God and relying on ourselves. It started in the garden. We, just as Adam and Eve, think we can run our lives better than God. Look where that has gotten us.

Quit trying to work your way to heaven. Quit trying to clean yourself up enough to get there. Stop thinking you are God and you can do it alone. Release the guilt that you are too bad and just simply receive the gift called grace through faith in Jesus Christ. Turn your life over to Him and then hang on and enjoy the ride. It's worth it. Do you have the gift of God?

Robbie's comments:

Salvation is one of those words that we Christians throw around and assume everyone understands. The Merriam-Webster Dictionary defines salvation as "deliverance from the power and effects of sin". The power and effects of sin is death. Romans 6:23 tells us that the wages of sin is death. But the deliverance from this is found in a relationship with Jesus Christ. This deliverance is offered to us as a free gift. We haven't earned it, we don't deserve it, and we will never fully understand it. But God loves us that much. God is our Creator, but doesn't become our Father until we accept this free gift. We then become His children and can start that relationship that He longs for us to have with Him. The gift is free, but if we don't pick up the gift and unwrap it, we will never get to experience all its splendor and glory. My prayer is that if you have not accepted this free gift, you will do that now. God wants you to accept this gift He is offering. He will never force you to accept it. Love is a choice and He wants you to accept it because you want to. It will be the greatest gift you have ever, or will ever, receive.

Jim's comments:

I understood this concept very early in my walk. I never thought for one minute there was anything I could ever offer God. I quickly realized the gift was free and gladly accepted it. Now, being as hard headed as I am, it took a little longer to turn my life completely over to Him. Just like the Bible says, He disciplines those He loves and He finally disciplined me into submission around January 16th, 2006.

Are You Committing Adultery?

Matthew 5:27-28 "You have heard that it was said, 'YOU SHALL NOT COMMIT ADULTERY'; but I say to you that everyone who looks at a woman with lust for her has already committed adultery with her in his heart".

I want to say up front I am not talking about the physical act of adultery. My heart goes out to all of those hurt by adultery. God has forgiven them and I pray they will forgive themselves, forgive others and seek other's forgiveness. I want to talk about what Jesus calls adultery and how that leads to the physical act.

It all starts in the mind. It starts with that thought we don't take captive. Men who take that second long look and then start to picture her in various stages of undress. Or, it could be as simple as she understands you when your wife doesn't. Once the fantasy takes hold in your mind, it then proceeds to the heart. You start to notice your wife's flaws and then you block out what brought you together in the first place. This is what Jesus is talking about. It is all the thoughts that lead up to the actual act. It starts in the mind, goes to the heart, and ends up in bed.

For women it may be different. It may not be totally physical but an emotional attraction. He compliments you. He pays attention to you. He listens. He seems to be a caring person. All the things your husband is not. Again, she focuses on her husband's defects while seeing nothing but the good side in Mr. Perfect. It may even be he is more successful than her husband. It starts in the mind, goes to the heart, and ends up in bed.

The only way to protect yourself is to take every thought captive. Communicate openly and deeply with your spouse. Read what God's Word says about infidelity and divorce. Have an accountability partner of the same sex who will ask the tough questions. Try to avoid any situation where you will be alone with someone of the opposite sex. You commit adultery in the mind and heart long before you take it to the physical act. A lot of people have committed adultery in their hearts and minds without every taking it to the physical act and it still leaves scars. Stay in the Word and stay committed.

Focus on your spouse's good qualities and keep your heart and mind from lusting after others. Are you committing adultery?

Robbie's comments:

There was a time in my life when I would have said that it was OK for a married woman or man to have a friend of the opposite sex. I had them, but no more. I have turned a complete 180 on this topic. I know how relationships develop. I have seen it happen too many times to think for one minute that a man and woman can only be friends. If you are married and have a close friend of the opposite sex, be careful, be very careful. If you are married and know that your spouse has a close friend of the opposite sex, be careful, be very careful. My real advice is to nip it in the bud. There is no good that can come from it. I would be interested to see how many extra marital affairs started out as "just friends". Men and women were designed to be attracted to one another and if given enough time alone together, they will bond. Did your relationship with your spouse start off as a friendship that developed into something deeper as you spent more time together? That's what happens when two people spend time together. They bond. We all need close friends. Just make sure they are of the same sex.

Jim's comments:

Again, in my former life I looked upon women as sex objects but not any more. We as men are visual and a woman can get my attention. The key is for me to not take the second glance and I am very good at not doing so. I had the opportunity to live with eight other guys for three weeks recently and most were not believers and the way they talked about women, sometimes their own women, was appalling. Most were probably faithful and it was just "guy" talk but that is how it starts.

Are You Still Under Law?

Hebrews 8:7,13 For if that first covenant had been faultless, there would have been no occasion sought for a second. (13)When He said, "A new covenant," He has made the first obsolete But whatever is becoming obsolete and growing old is ready to disappear.

The Law, confusing to some, dismissed by others, but what exactly is it? In its simplest terms it is a list of do's and don'ts and the consequences of not doing the dos or doing the don'ts. It was God's measuring stick for His people. It is a covenant between Him and them that they could not live up to. That is why He initiated the second, or New Covenant.

The Law in itself is not bad. If everyone obeyed it we would have a perfect world. It was designed to show us that we can't live up to it. We can't keep the Law and be righteous enough to come into the presence of a Holy God. It did what it was designed to do, which was to show us we need a Savior.

Now, are you still under the Law? Do you have to do certain rituals and obey specific commandments to stay saved? Is your salvation in jeopardy if you have a bad day? Have you lost your salvation one day and then worked hard to get it back the next? If you are in Christ Jesus you are under grace and cannot lose your salvation. The moral part of the Law should not be dismissed because it is how God wishes we would act. There is a lot of good in some of the dos and don'ts, but they can't save you. Are you still under Law?

Robbie's comments:

Thank God I am not! If I had to go to bed each night wondering if I had done enough that day to keep my salvation, I would not only drive myself crazy, but I am sure I would fail miserably! I have no doubt that I fall short every day of doing all that I can to further the Kingdom. And then I would constantly wonder, "What is enough"? I'm sure my "enough" wouldn't look like your "enough". How totally frustrating would that be? The Bible is full of dos and don'ts that we should no doubt be paying attention to and striving for. They are there to help us live d.u.I. Will we ever be perfect? No, but we should be trying each and every day to look more like Christ, who was perfect. The great thing about grace is that we never have to worry about losing our salvation once we have accepted what Christ did on the cross for us. He covered our sins with His blood and it is done.

Jim's comments:

I don't "have" to do certain things but there are certain things I like to do and feel the need to do them on a daily basis to remain close to Him, but not to stay saved. I know I am saved by grace and the things I do are based on my gratitude, not salvation, and that is the key. As long as I understand why I am doing something and that grace is free I will be okay. I am sure some people will say this book is "legalistic" because of all the times we say "you need to do this or that" but this is not for salvation. These suggestions are based on our own experiences and watching others. If you continue your walk the same way you always have, you will get the same results you always have.

Where Do You Get Your Wisdom?

James 1:5 But if any of you lacks wisdom, let him ask of God, who gives to all generously and without reproach, and it will be given to him.

Do you have street smarts or book smarts? Do you have a degree or a diploma? Do you use common sense or do you do everything by trial and error? Regardless of what you study or how much you study, it's still all information. Wisdom is much, much more. Wisdom is more about judgment, discernment and knowing the difference between right and wrong. It cannot be learned from a book. It comes from God.

God is the author of wisdom. It is His nature and it is in His Word. It is brought to us by the Holy Spirit. He can give it to us by reading His Word, through other's experiences or direct revelation. The key to getting wisdom is to ask God and then listen. He even has a whole book of the Bible (Proverbs) dedicated to wisdom.

On the other hand, you can try to get wisdom on your own. You can read books, take advice from the world, and do what everyone else does. That's not wisdom and it leads down the wrong path. The world's ways and God's ways are not the same. Wisdom comes from God and is His alone. All you have to do is ask. Where do you get your wisdom?

Robbie's comments:

I started reading Proverbs every day again a few months ago. Isn't it funny how each time you read God's Word you will learn something, or read something, or get an understanding of something, that you never had before? Proverbs was one of those books that I would read but it really was just words. Every now and then, I would have a "wow" moment but nothing very life changing. Well, this time was the first time I read Proverbs and every single chapter was a "wow" chapter. I really hated that I rushed through it by reading a chapter each day. Each chapter was filled with so much. I really want to do a more in depth study on each chapter and hopefully will start that soon. The wisdom that oozes from the pages of Proverbs has just been amazing this time around. It is full of dos and don'ts. Some are repeated over and over again. I figure things are repeated over and over again in the Bible because we must need to hear them over and over again. I have gained both wisdom and knowledge and pray I will continue being diligent in my search for both.

Jim's comments:

This is what I love about God's Word; it is where wisdom can be found. Reading His Word and asking Him for wisdom is the only way to get it. I can tell how much people read God's word by the choices they make. Wisdom comes from Him and Him alone and that is where I get mine.

Are You A Christian?

Act 2:42 They were continually devoting themselves to the apostles' teaching and to fellowship, to the breaking of bread and to prayer.

I need to state first and foremost that I am not stating a doctrine of works. Christianity is not a check list of things you do to achieve salvation or to keep it. Just because you read your Bible (apostles teaching), hang out with Christians (fellowship), break bread (the Lords Supper), and pray does not make you a Christian. On the other hand, if you have no desire to do any of these, I would have to doubt your conversion. If you are truly born again and indwelt with the Holy Spirit you will be drawn to God's Word. You would desire to read it so as to know Him better. You would want to attend and serve in a good Bible teaching church and be around other believers. You would want to bring to remembrance what Christ did to set you free. How can you say you have a relationship with the Father if you don't talk with Him through prayer?

This verse describes the very first church. This was how the church was created. It was created by God, through individuals who were born of the Holy Spirit. It wasn't formed by a committee, not by some splitting off because of doctrinal issues, not because the members got baptized, not because of confirmation, not because they met on the right day, not because they spoke in tongues, not because they believed in the latter saints, but because they believed in the death, burial, and resurrection of Jesus Christ and received the Holy Spirit. PERIOD!

Verse 41 reads "that day 3,000 were added". The first day of the church 3,000 people were convicted and converted. Then came discipleship. When someone is converted and not taught, growth comes at a very slow pace. The early church realized this and set a plan in motion. Continually devoted to the apostles' teaching does not mean one hour on Sunday morning. If you are truly born again you will desire to feed on God's Word. You will want to be around your brothers and sisters in Christ. You will desire to serve your King and talk to Him through prayer. I have heard people say Christianity is a personal relationship, which it is, but it should bring about a change in you that is very public.

Brian Hendrix, my Sunday School teacher always says, "When things in my life are going wrong I go back to Acts 2:42 and see which one of the four are being neglected; prayer, fellowship, Lord's Supper, or Bible study". Again I want to state doing these does not make you a Christian, but check your relationship with Him if you have no desire to do any of them. Are you a Christian?

Robbie's comments:

Yes, I am. I have no doubt. I think there are a lot of Christians that have made a decision to start that relationship with Christ but nobody ever took the time to show them "what next?" When Paul would go to a city and start a church, he didn't just leave after some decided to believe. He left others in charge to continue the teaching and discipleship. We have to be in a good Bible study if we want to grow in Christ. I'm not saying it's not important to read the Bible and study on your own, but left to our own devices we could get into some trouble. When we get with other believers and a good teacher either our interpretation will be confirmed or corrected. Either way, we will have dug deeper and gained a greater understanding. Usually, when we are not growing and we don't have that zeal and excitement like we used to, we are either not attending church regularly, not praying consistently, not spending time with other believers or not involved in a good Bible study. If you are a Christian, I hope you are doing all these things. If not, I would encourage you to get the right balance in your life and in your Christian walk. We don't want to be walking around lopsided. More importantly, we don't want to be walking around discouraged or frustrated.

Jim's comments:

I believe this book and the ministry speak for themselves on the importance I place on this verse in the believer's life!

Conclusion

Well, how did you do? Our prayer is that you understand your faith a little better and how to grow that faith so as to please God. We hope you have the gift of God and that you are a Christian. We hope you have learned to keep your mouth from getting you in trouble and not to judge by appearance.

Is your "yes" yes and you don't gossip? Are you careful how you look at the opposite sex? Are you dwelling on the goodness of God and getting your wisdom from Him? When you have the Lord's Supper it's not out of legalism, is it? Our prayer is that you would use this book over and over again, maybe using a journal, to take a spiritual inventory to help you be more like Christ. Our goal is instruction with love and we hope we have achieved that. God bless!

A Final Thought

Robbie's final thought:

I pray that this book has touched you as much by reading it as it has me by us writing it. I just want every believer to walk daily under the influence of the Holy Spirit and in the victory that Christ died to give us. I hope this book has helped you reach that next level in your walk. Being a Christian comes with responsibilities if we want to truly experience the abundant life. This book was designed to help you in your journey. The journey lasts a lifetime. We never arrive but must continue towards the goal each and every day.

I want to encourage each of you to remember the church in Acts 2:42. Remember, it's all about balance. Read God's Word, fellowship with other brothers and sisters in Christ, get in or continue in a good Bible study and remember Christ by partaking of the Lord's Supper. Continue to encourage one another to live d.u.I.!

Jim's final thought:

God is good! (All the time)! All the time! (God is good)! This is what we as believers should be shouting as we walk through this world. He is good and when we stop and reflect on His goodness it should make us want to serve Him with excellence. My prayer is that you are tired of hearing about what God has done in the past or what He might do in the future. And I pray you are ready to experience Him now and that you are ready to delve into that deep, personal relationship which, although it does require work, is totally satisfying and fulfilling. It's what you have been longing for in your walk. It's what He made you for. It's about **being** a Christian, not just acting like one.

I also hope some of you have come to that personal knowledge of who Christ is. I have seen many church goers who think they are Christians and who will be sadly disappointed come judgment day. Please don't make that mistake. I don't know if you have really turned your life over to Christ and accepted His work on the cross, but I know **YOU** do. Please take some time to reflect on your life and be **SURE** you are His. We never know when we will breathe our last breath. If you are truly His, I will see you all one day in heaven!

How To Contact Us

d.u.I. ministries offers: Speaking engagements: Teaching Seminars, Church Planting, and/or Starting a Prayer Partners Ministry at your church.

Please contact us at P.O. Box 1239 Fairview, TN 37062, duiministries@quixnet.net, or www.duiministries.com.

Printed in the United States
152031LV00005B/3/P